About the Author

Currently an assistant
at the State Universi
Fredonia, Marvin Lu
Ph.D. from New York University. He
previously taught at Rutgers University,
the City College of New York, and at the
overseas division of the University of
Maryland. He has also been a lecturer on
Iberian history at the New School of
Social Research in New York City.

The Council of the
Santa Hermandad

Leyes dela hermādad.

¶ Este es el quaderno delas le
yes nueuas ōla hermādad del rey ⁊ dela reyna nōs
señoꝛes:y poꝛ su mādado becbas enla jūta general
entoꝛdelaguna:notificadas el año del nascimiēto
de nōo saluadoꝛ jesu xꝓo de mil.cccc.⁊.lꝛꝛꝛvj.años.

Title page of The Laws of the Brotherhood,
a sixteen page book printed in 1520

THE COUNCIL OF THE
SANTA HERMANDAD

A Study of the Pacification Forces

of Ferdinand and Isabella

by Marvin Lunenfeld

UNIVERSITY OF MIAMI PRESS
Coral Gables, Florida

Contents

Illustrations

Introduction

NO PART of the Castilian government aroused more fear during the fifteenth century than the royal police force of the *Santa Hermandad*. For centuries the Holy Brotherhood's jurisdiction had been limited to guarding roads and patrolling wilderness areas outside the towns. Then Isabella I unleashed it upon her cities and allowed its judges to override the competence of ordinary courts. Trial was arbitrary, appeal difficult, and penalties severe—death by an arrow through the heart was a common sentence. In little time the queen's dominions were pacified and dissent was silenced.

The queen's subjects were not the only ones to feel the weight of brotherhood arms. Isabella hurled them against the Portuguese, who had embroiled themselves in Castile's War of Succession (1474–1479) by supporting her rival to the throne. That struggle was successful and on its heels came another, a grinding war against the Moorish kingdom of Granada. By the war's end, the brotherhood forces had blossomed into a full-scale army, a predecessor of the royal Spanish infantry that bestrode Europe for a century.

During the last of the fifteenth century the brotherhood's operation was conducted in the queen's interest by a royal governing board, the Council of the Santa Hermandad (hereafter referred to as the Council). Before exploring the relationship between the Council and the crown, it is necessary to understand the history of the Council and of the brotherhood it dominated.

During the High Middle Ages Castilian cities formed alliances called brotherhoods (*hermandades*) to protect their rights and advance their prosperity. In moments of severe governmental crisis these leagues blossomed into kingdomwide unions, the general brotherhoods (*hermandades generales*). They governed themselves by means of an administrative committee elected by a delegate assembly. Troops were raised by each municipality and pooled within provinces as a militia for the common defense under one supreme commander. These great leagues were temporary, to be resorted to in time of emergency. The leagues tended to respect royal authority, and, indeed, Castile's kings at times actively promoted their creation.

In peacetime the general brotherhoods disbanded, and control over the fighting men reverted to the cities where they were raised. These troops evolved into permanent police forces. Each force was composed of a small governing council, *alcaldes* (justices of the peace), and squads of mounted crossbowmen. In normal times police duties were limited to the protection of roads and rural areas, but the brotherhood's fighting men were always available to fight under the banner of a great league if a call were issued.

The best known of the general brotherhoods was developed by the Catholic Sovereigns, Ferdinand and Isabella, during the Castilian War of Succession. To assure some measure of control over this league its governing body was made over into a royal Council by Isabella. This was the first time a monarch directly brought a brotherhood structure into government. The president of this new Council was the bishop of Cartagena, Lope de Ribas, a trusted advisor to the queen. Finance was entrusted to Isabella's treasury officers, Alfonso de Quintanilla and Juan de Ortega, who supervised the setting and collecting of taxes. Alonso de Palencia was named attorney general. To insure the loyalty of the military, command went to Ferdinand's natural brother, Alfonso de Aragón. The constable of Castile, Pedro Fernandez de Velasco, and a prominent judge, Gonzalo Sanchez de Illescas, were in time given seats, bringing to seven the full Council membership. These principal officers and their small staff of accountants, scribes, and legists ran brotherhood affairs in the queen's interests. They had the duty of administering a kingdomwide network of rural police. This proved no small task. The police were always given jurisdiction over crimes of arson, murder, rape, and robbery that were committed in the wilderness and on highways. After 1476 their jurisdiction was dramatically broadened under royal guidance to include populated areas and all punishment of rebels against the crown.

The Council also had to oversee the formation and maintenance of a militia, a fighting force separate from the police, which was raised on a provincial basis by the populace of Castile. Although at first this militia consisted of only a few thousand cavalrymen and footsoldiers with their officers, it made a useful contribution to Isabella during the civil war. Council direction of militia and police gave the young queen a means of pacifying her enemies and extending her power into the cities.

The long war against the kingdom of Granada (1481–1492) brought a fundamental shift in Council interests. The Council slowly divested itself of police supervision in order to concentrate upon expanding the militia. This militia, which grew to over 10,000 men, served with distinction until at last a cross rose over the Alhambra. Peaceful years followed and the militia was dismantled. Using the experience gained from supervising the brotherhood militia, the Council performed its last service for the queen in 1496 by recruiting and training a royal infantry. Two years later, Isabella, maintaining that the league had completed its tasks, disbanded the Council and entirely released the police from the discipline of crown-appointed officials. Some cities accepted the choice of continuing in small hermandades and for several centuries more their police forces continued to function as road and wilderness patrols, long after the Catholic Sovereigns passed into glorious memory.

The Council has long attracted interest as an early manifesta-
tion of the monarchs' centralizing zeal. Along with the accumula-
tion of the grandmasterships of the military orders, the domination
of the sheepherders' Mesta, and the creation of the Inquisition, it
is considered to be a major example of Ferdinand and Isabella's
move toward national consolidation.

Traditional theories about Isabella's power base adhere to certain interpretations of the function of the Council. According to
standard interpretation, acceptance of a royal governing body for
the league was a prime example of burgher support for a strong
monarchy. Active cooperation of the townsmen was imperative;
how otherwise could the queen have organized and coordinated
police work? Without the help of the townsmen a national organization would have been impossible, the number of administrators
alone precluding it. The assistance of the burghers has been ex-
plained by presuming that they wanted a monarchy pledged to
protect them, especially from the powerful grandees. Crown and
city together used the Santa Hermandad to launch an attack on
the rebellious nobility, a cause of Castile's anarchy. The successful
intimidation of the aristocracy has been held to have strengthened
the monarchy and favored the bourgeois.

The brotherhood continues to be viewed as it was first presented by Isabella's chroniclers: an institution created by her to
intimidate powerful subjects and overcome lawlessness and anarchy. It is also still presumed, even by the authoritative scholar
Tarsicio de Azcona, that the Council gave Isabella control of every
detail of the brotherhoods.[1] J. H. Elliot, another well-known authority, repeats the traditional thesis that the Santa Hermandad
was under unified central control.[2]

As with other aspects of the reign of Ferdinand and Isabella,
this picture of efficient despotism can be overdrawn. The Catholic
Sovereigns were vigorous personalities and astute propagandists,
and many scholars have expressed belief that they were "New
Monarchs," qualitatively different from their predecessors. An examination of the Council of the Santa Hermandad suggests that

this belief may be derived not from actions but from clever royal statements of intent, from household chroniclers, and from Ferdinand and Isabella's sense of the dramatic.

A reinterpretation of the aims, the organization, and the achievements of the Holy Brotherhood is needed. Despite widespread interest in the Holy Brotherhood, no analysis has been undertaken of the important governing Council.

This work attempts to provide a more complete picture of the activities of the Holy Brotherhood and its governing Council. Examination of unpublished papers in archives in Spain yields convincing evidence that traditional ideas regarding the creation, composition, and achievements of the Council must be revised.

The starting point for my reevaluation is in the books of ordinances in manuscript in the archives of Simancas and the National Library of Madrid. Going far beyond the often consulted chronicles and Cortes proceedings, they give new insight into the creation and growth of the brotherhood. The archives of Simancas and Seville yielded correspondence from the Council to the queen's subjects that permits an estimation of the degree of control over subordinates. National fiscal policy was reconstructed from budget fragments in the archives of Simancas. Provincial dealings with the Council are recorded in municipal archives in Seville and Burgos. Ledger books and other documents for the city of Ciudad Real, which are preserved in the National Historical Archives of Madrid, allowed for a shift in perspective from the royal to the local level.

I have been aided in my research by the guidance and kindness of friends and librarians in the United States and in Spain. I owe particular thanks to Dr. Ángel de La Plaza Bores, vice-director of the Archives of Simancas, and his staff. I appreciate the aid of the personnel of the Municipal Archives of Seville, Burgos, and Toledo, the National Library and National Historical Archives of Madrid, and the library of the Hispanic Institute of New York.

Since Professor David L. Hicks of New York University first kindled my interest in the Spanish side of the Renaissance era, he has been not only a keen guide to the historian's craft but an unflinching critic. His help has been particularly valuable to me and I wish to acknowledge my gratitude. I especially appreciate the assistance and encouragement of Profesor John E. Fagg and Professor Marshall W. Baldwin of New York University, and Professor Guillermo Céspedes del Castillo of the University of Seville. Professor A. H. De Oliveira Marques read a draft of the manuscript and made a number of important suggestions. Valuable criticism regarding Castilian taxation was offered by Professor Nicholás Sánchez-Albornoz. All the readers are due my gratitude; any errors remain, of course, my responsibility.

To my wife, Katharine, I am indebted for the preservation of a joyful life midst the distractions of research and writing.

The Council of the Santa Hermandad

1

Origins of the Brotherhood

ALL communities are concerned with the protection of life and property. In medieval times these functions were discharged in Muslim cities by the Shurta, an urban militia-police. This repressive instrument, which appeared in Spain in the ninth century, enacted prompt and harsh justice.[1] During the centuries of the Reconquest of Muslim Spain, the Christians fell heir to important Islamic cities. The Muslim police may have been the inspiration for a Christian imitation.[2]

Although there are obscure records from as early as 1100 that hint at primitive city police in Christian areas,[3] the first good documentation for municipal police guilds (*cofradía* and *germanitate*) dates from the mid-thirteenth century.[4] The term hermandad appears in Castile at about the same time. Luis Suárez Fernández states that Castilians reserved the term hermandad for organizations with wider implications than mere police duty.[5] He found several groups called by the name brotherhood in the middle ages: religious fraternities, which do not concern us, and three municipal organizations: (1) the little studied *hermandad de la marina de Castilla,* a stable league of northern mercantile cities with common economic interests, (2) the *Hermandad Vieja de Toledo,* a permanent corps of guards maintained by property owners to protect their goods, and (3) the *hermandades generales de Castilla y León*.[6]

This last group slowly evolved from temporary leagues of cities preoccupied with political and economic cooperation in unsettled times into a national police force primarily concerned with maintaining order in the wilderness. The earliest known *hermandad general* dates from about 1200 among the brotherhoods of Escalona and Avila, Segovia, and Plasencia.[7] The step from small-scale leagues for mutual advantage to a kingdomwide union of municipalities was a great one, not as yet clearly understood. Suárez Fernández demonstrates convincingly that the first such kingdomwide union was instituted by Alfonso X's rebellious son Sancho IV at the Cortes of 1282 in order to usurp his father's throne.[8] This Cortes created four simultaneous brotherhoods (religious orders, clergy, nobility, and urban). The municipal one was a simple union whose members met in an annual assembly. There was an administrative committee, but no magistrate had more power than the members. The cities joined together primarily to defend their privileges, and, although initiated by royalty, retained independence.[9]

When Sancho died in 1295 a number of municipal leagues were spontaneously revived to suppress the anarchy and confusion attendant upon the minority succession of Ferdinand IV. Leagues were born for Castile, Galicia with Leon, and Toledo with Extremadura; all were confirmed at the 1295 Cortes of Valladolid.[10]

The permutations of the leagues will not be examined in detail until the reign of Henry IV, but it should be noted that marked advances in structure took place in 1295. Deputies transacted business under a common seal. Fixed meeting places were established (e.g., Leon, Burgos) that became true capitals for the general brotherhoods.[11] Total independence from outside control of the cities in this league was then gradually lost. After several years of civil war, during which time the cities had fallen prey to noble factions, a powerful league was again created at the Cortes of Burgos in 1315.[12] After the emergency passed that called this league into existence, the individualism of the municipal governments once again asserted itself. There is no record of a league active between 1325 and 1370. When next reported they have been transformed by the Trastamara dynasty from commercial leagues into a force of rural police, after the example of the Hermandad Vieja de Toledo.[13]

The Hermandad Vieja was an association of property owners that maintained a corps of armed guards for the protection of estates.[14] The essential elements of the organization were: regular councils at which all members met to promulgate and enforce regulations; alcaldes to keep documents and render justice; *cuad-rilleros* (squads of archers) to arrest and execute malefactors. Although in principle only a league of persons, it developed into a quasi-governmental military force. The crown fostered the association because of royal interest in the archers.[15]

At the Cortes of Valladolid in 1351, Peter I made an abortive start towards revising the general brotherhoods in the norms of the Hermandad Vieja, only to be toppled soon after.[16] It was left to his rival, Enrique de Trastamara, to effectuate the change. In 1370 he convoked the Cortes at Medina del Campo for a new formation of the general brotherhoods, not disdaining to use as the league's new constitution the ordinances of 1351.[17] The transformation was not complete, as the king still gave his cities liberty to set up their brotherhoods in the form most convenient to them.[18]

The House of Trastamara arrived at a critical moment in its history in 1386. John I faced a threat from the king of Portugal and an invasion through Galicia by the duke of Lancaster, pretender to his throne. The Castilian municipalities were loyal to their king and hurried to his aid. The result was the definitive 1386 constitution of the Cortes of Segovia,[19] wherein the general brotherhood was made uniform throughout the kingdoms and given the task of maintaining internal security.[20] From then until the reign of Isabella, each revival of a general brotherhood re-adopted the 1386 constitution with only slight modification.[21]

By the mid-fifteenth century the hermandades had taken on the characteristics that marked their later incarnations. General brotherhoods were temporary, to be resorted to only in times of governmental breakdown. They tended to be respectful of royal authority and to exert their influence to restore stability during minority successions or invasions.

During the interminable civil wars of the fifteenth century, however, the brotherhoods did not present a united front. Urban solidarity was broken by noble infiltration into municipal government, and the brotherhoods fell prey to factionalism. It was this fatal lack of cohesion, well-illustrated during the reign of Henry IV (1454–1474), that accounts for the ease with which Ferdinand and Isabella were able to capture control of a sizable number of brotherhoods in the opening stages of the War of Succession.

It has been popularly held by historians that the general brotherhoods fell into disuse before 1476, and Isabella breathed new life into a dead body.[22] Examination of her predecessor's kingship reveals, however, that the brotherhood was in no need of resuscitation. Leagues flourished thanks to Henry IV's troubles. King Henry faced his most serious challenge in 1465 when a band of rebellious grandees broke into open rebellion under the leadership of the marquis of Villena and his uncle, the archbishop of Toledo.

In a curious ceremony, held on a broad field near Avila on July 5, 1465, these nobles "deposed" Henry by knocking down an effigy of the king from a mock throne and then crowning Henry's half brother, the young Alfonso, who took his place on the vacant seat.[23] As matters could hardly be settled that easily, armed conflict followed. Neither side had many regular troops and so wooed the city militias. Brotherhoods took to arms throughout the kingdom in 1466, some favoring Henry, some favoring Alfonso, some neutral, but all united in their desire to hold down violent unaffiliated men who profited from anarchy.

In September 1467, representatives from cities, towns, and hamlets favorable to Henry met in Castronuño, a little village outside Valladolid, to draw up ordinances for a league to be named the "Holy Brotherhood of the Kingdoms of Castile and Leon."[24] These "Ordinances of Castronuño," only another re-drafting of the norms of 1386,[25] called for the municipal brotherhoods of each designated province to elect eight alcaldes as delegates to provincial assemblies.[26] The coordination and direction of these provincial bodies was to be entrusted to delegates who, along with all other brotherhood officials, high and low, would meet together in a *Junta General* (General Assembly). The mandates of the league were to be carried out by the executive officer, the *Capitán Superior Mayor* (Supreme Commander), named by the body to direct the provincial captains and their fighting men. At the municipal level the league's business was administered by two or more alcaldes who were empowered to collect revenue, build jails, define and limit their own juridical jurisdiction, and try cases.[27] They were given areas of criminal jurisdiction (*casos*) that were extremely broadly drafted: all crimes committed on the roads or in unpopulated areas; rape of honest women; blasphemy; and the passing of false money.[28] Because the league enjoyed the backing of the crown and of loyal nobles, it forcibly collected revenue from recalcitrant cities and kept local order.[29]

The king played a minor role in forming and regulating this league. Even friendly chronicles do not suggest that he was ever a prime mover. A letter sent to the village of Tordesillas regarding the brotherhood illuminates Henry's passive attitude. After a lengthy opening regarding the blessings of God in reducing great tyrants and adventurers, mentioning in passing Jeremiah's captivity and the destruction of Jerusalem by the Savior, the king lamented, "Oh disconsolate earth covered with evildoing." The brotherhood was then congratulated for keeping the peace, multiplying goodness, and honoring virtue against the profaners and persecutors, the scandal of the fatherland. In closing he exhorted the city to come to his aid: "For should you not go, Castile will cease to be. Should you not rouse yourself her ruin is certain."[30]

Henry was unable to hold this league together for very long in the face of his aristocratic opponents. Yet the entire high nobility did not object to the league. Clear proof of this is shown by a pact of union signed between the cities and villages of Castile (which met in General Assembly at Burgos in July 1468) and the following grandees: Alvaro de Zúñiga, count of Palencia, Diego Hurtado de Mendoza, marques of Santillana, and Pedro Fernandez de Valasco, count of Haro.[31]

Fortunately for these men and their king, the pretender Alfonso died in 1468 leaving no acceptable alternative to Henry. The rebellious faction tried offering its support to Doña Isabella, but she, acting alone or with the prompting of advisors, declined the offer and made a settlement with the king, her half brother, that returned peace to Castile.[32] Henry's opponents were at least able to accomplish one objective: bringing down the league, an action that proved in accord with typical city mistrust of centralized authority. At the Cortes of Ocaña in 1469 a petition was presented charging that the funds raised for Henry's brotherhood were being squandered and diverted to his own pockets.[33] The General Assembly dissolved, and the brotherhood collapsed into several smaller leagues.[34]

With Isabella's marriage in 1469 to Ferdinand, son of Henry's enemy, John II of Aragon, the uneasy truce was broken. Although the newlyweds kept a surface peace with the king they went about organizing a strong power base in anticipation of the future.[35]

With equal anticipation the king's supporters proposed the revival of a general brotherhood.[36] In July 1473 the reconstituted league held its first General Assembly in Villacastin, where ordinances were drawn up for the "New General Brotherhood of the Kingdoms of Castile and Leon."[37] The structure of earlier general brotherhoods was repeated but with a dramatic addition that the new charter proclaimed the most important of all duties was defense of the king.[38]

It is evident from this capsule history that when Henry IV

died on December 11, 1474, Ferdinand and Isabella did not have to delve into the distant past to discover that the municipalities had a powerful fighting machine in their brotherhoods. The general brotherhoods changed, in the three centuries reviewed, from an ad hoc league constituted in a vital moment of municipal, political, and economic expansion, into a stable body of uniformed rural police.

2

The Brotherhood and the Castilian Municipalities, 1474-1479

TRADITIONAL interpretations of Isabella's reign by the romantic historians presented her as an impoverished young queen who ascended her throne faced with a rebellion. She obtained the eagerly given assistance of her commons and together an alliance was worked out of crown and municipality. This alliance effectively suppressed social anarchy (Isabella's legacy from her predecessor, the weak Henry IV), and brought low the impudent, rebellious Castilian magnates. Her reign provided nineteenth century authors with an excellent example of a "Renaissance despot" who skillfully gathered all power into her hands and would have laid the groundwork for a unified, modern state if not for the errors of her descendants. Although this old-fashioned picture is simplistic, it still holds great sway despite new research that has undermined favorite theories of another era.[1]

One of the most important revisions is of the view of the civil war that followed upon the death of Henry IV of Castile. The two contenders for his throne were Doña Juana, presumed by her suporters to be the king's daughter, and Henry's half-sister Doña Isabella. Juana has long borne the slanderous nickname of *La Beltraneja* since she was reputed by some to be the issue of the king's second wife, Juana of Portugal, by a favorite, Don Beltran de la Cueva. Henry's reputation as a weakling and a sexual deviate gave popular credence to this rumor.

It is, however, no longer tenable to maintain without reservation that Juana could not possibly be the king's daughter or that he did not intend that she succeed him. A massive campaign of propaganda and falsification directed against Henry and his child has been uncovered by J. B. Stiges,[2] Gregorio Marañón,[3] Orestes Ferrara,[4] and, especially, Jaime Vicens Vives.[5] Isabella was able to create an official history of the succession after successfully seizing full control of the state apparatus, but the most authoritative historians writing in modern times on the Reyes Católicos deny that she had primacy to Castile's throne.[6]

Continuing to explain Isabella's relations with Castilian municipalities simply as those of a lawful monarch and her loyal subjects cooperating to put down traitorous supporters of Juana fails to take into account altered views of the succession struggle. The reason for her success in dominating the towns might be found in other areas. The municipalities of Castile were unable to present a united front against a determined Isabella because they were entrenched in isolationism. The cities of the interior had failed to see advantages in lasting commercial alliances and, except for infrequent military leagues of their hermandades, they remained isolated from one another. The Cortes, which once gave cities a powerful voice in the land, was in an advanced state of decay and had few weapons left with which to extort concessions in return for cooperation.

New studies show as well that the governments of some of these cities were unstable. Municipal liberties that had been the pride of Castile's cities in the twelfth and thirteenth centuries no longer protected them from noble or royal intrusion into their independence. From the reign of John II municipal offices were sold in direct contravention of the ancient charters. Key municipal officers, such as alcaldes, were very often crown appointees or were displaced by *corregidors* (royal overseers).[7] An extremely unstable municipal judicial system also provided ample opportunities for the crown to advance its cause or the cause of favored bodies like the Mesta.[8] These conflicting pressures played havoc with municipal government. Eloy Benito Ruano's *Toledo en el siglo XV: Vida politica* provides an excellent study of the tangle of rival factions that struggled for control of the municipal governing corporation and for the allegiance of the lower classes.[9] Benito Ruano points out that in Toledo, high and low nobility, merchants, New Christians, Jews, and demagogue-led masses jostled for advantage. In other cities stability among factions was often purchased at the price of oligarchy. L. P. Serrano shows that this was the case with Burgos.[10] The city was ruled by a tight, self-perpetuating municipal corporation that was a model for much of Castile. Ferdinand and Isabella's success in manipulating the cities hinged upon their ability to mete out awards and punishments to different factions in each metropolis. Intensive archival research is needed to establish these points, but lacking this, some generalities on the treatment of segments of the urban population can be presented.

The nobility received most of the monetary rewards, leaving little but rhetoric to satisfy the rest of the population. Factions in these cities carried out the king and queen's goals not simply through a wholehearted spirit of cooperation but often because of a masterful blend of emotional appeals, promises, and coercion. Elaborate shows were made of royal ceremonies and processions to impress upon the populace the dignity and majesty of their new sovereigns. Grandiose religious spectacles were organized, especially to spur the struggle against the Moors.

The Cortes, principal instrument of urban political power, was lied to and awed. In 1476, immediately after the indecisive battle of Peleagonzalo, Ferdinand and Isabella hailed the result as a great victory and called a Cortes at Madrigal. The newly created prestige was used to gain municipal support from their allies of their full program (which included the Holy Brotherhood). The monarchs did not hesitate to break promises made to their commons. In this Cortes Isabella promised that she would heed the urban representatives' complaints that corregidors were being sent into cities without their consent. By the Cortes of 1480 she was secure enough to disregard this promise and freely sent her representatives into all the free cities of Castile.[11] Lies were not reserved for her dealings with the Cortes. In 1475 Isabella renewed all the privileges and exemptions granted by Henry IV to Toledo,[12] but the city's special "perpetual" exemptions from several taxes lasted only until the crown's power was consolidated.[13] The monarchs also had a variety of economic weapons available to keep their cities in line. Taxes were impounded, merchandise was blockaded, and there were threats to abrogate duty-free rights at fairs.

The picture that emerges from reviewing relations between the crown and the cities is that no true partnership seems to have existed. The answer to Ferdinand and Isabella's successes is found in the decay of urban power and in the political talents of an aggressive monarchy. The way in which the crown was able to wrest control of the brotherhoods between 1474 and 1479 offers an excellent example of royal domination of urban life.

One of Isabella's initial problems was the same as that which faced previous Castilian sovereigns: how to gain soldiers at minimal expense. Fighting forces that Iberian subjects made available to their monarchs, even uncontested ones, had always been small. Paid royal guards occasionally supplied by the Cortes to John II and Henry IV had been inadequate. This was a problem common to ambitious fifteenth century European sovereigns.

One of Isabella's solutions was to adopt the ancient institution of the hermandades to her needs. The rural police offered her significant advantages if only they could be enticed to contribute men to her cause. They had trained archers who had long experience in suppressing crime. The formation of a general brotherhood in troubled times was considered a patriotic duty and its structure was suited to a country as sectional as Castile. Precedents for central control had already been laid, but in 1474 not all cities were willing to accept Isabella's rule and she was forced to move cautiously.

Upon the death of Henry IV the municipalities of Castile split between Juana and Isabella.[14] Ferdinand gave some thoughts in 1474 to creating a league for his wife's cities, but brotherhoods were not recruited in earnest until the following year when Afonso V of Portugal made a dramatic decision to take up Juana's cause and invade Castile.[15] Early in 1475, before Afonso made good on his threat, Ferdinand and Isabella met with their advisors in the great fortress at Burgos to fashion their league.[16] Based upon the events that followed, it is plausible to assume that the following simple plan was adopted: brotherhoods would be contacted in cities loyal to Isabella, a league would be formed, and at an opportune time a national body would be established to control the growth of the league.

After this meeting Juan de Ortega, a native of Burgos, and Alfonso de Quintanilla set out to promote the cause of Isabella's general brotherhood. They visited a number of towns and villages, including Palencia, Medina, Olmedo, Avila, Segovia, Salamanca, and Zamora, where they obtained the consent of important personages to send representatives to the anticipated convocation.[17] Meanwhile, Ferdinand and Isabella reconfirmed the charters of a number of brotherhoods.[18]

These troops were put to immediate use. A large number of the 12,000 cavalrymen and 30,000 infantrymen that assembled in 1475 at Valladolid and Tordesillas were probably members of the brotherhood.[19] In February 1476 Ferdinand arrived at Afonso's encampment in Zamora, across the Duero River from the city of Toro. The Portuguese attacked Zamora, but after an inconclusive siege Afonso withdrew. On the way back to his base he was overtaken by Ferdinand. The Portuguese drew up in battle formation on a plain to the east of Toro where ensued, at the beginning of March, the famous battle of Peleagonzalo.[20] Although this melee concluded without a clear victory for either side, Juana's prestige was badly damaged because Afonso did not carry the day for her.[21] Isabella seized this opportunity to make the war turn in her favor. It was time to strengthen her hold on Castile. A triumphant Cortes would be held.

This gathering opened at the end of March at Madrigal, a favored residence of Isabella not far from Valladolid.[22] The assemblage included the glittering range of Isabella's allies—great nobility, gentry, clerics, functionaries, and municipal delegates.[23] It was not difficult for Ferdinand and Isabella to manipulate this Cortes. The number of participants was small, and spectators were barred to keep the proceedings secret.[24] Debate was limited. Most business was done in writing as usual. Municipal representatives presented their petitions, which the sovereigns might transform into law by royal sanction or turn back to be modified or reversed. Though the crown might itself initiate the petition (as was the case with the brotherhood memorial) medieval men still had a strong need to comply with all outward forms.

The most important business enacted at the 1476 Cortes was the formal establishment of the new general brotherhood. A lengthy petition calling for a brotherhood was prepared some time before the end of March.[25] This petition, presented to the queen in the name of the delegates, complained about robbers, thieves, and murderers who infested the kingdom and protested the intrusion of Portugal into Castilian territory. It begged that the situation be resolved by the establishment of a brotherhood for all the kingdoms, and asked that "the order come from on high because then it will have the greater vigor and force."[26] Ferdinand and Isabella graciously accepted the petition on April 19 [27] and eight days later had it published as a royal ordinance.[28]

Every city, village, and hamlet was to join a brotherhood within thirty days. Structure and practices of these local police forces were drawn without much modification from previous reigns. The only discernible major revision for the rural police lay in the jurisdictions of alcaldes. Ferdinand and Isabella enumerated their judicial domain more specifically than previously thought necessary: highway crimes; murder or wounding of persons; robbery of goods; burning of houses, vines and fields; private imprisonment without proper authority. All of these crimes fell to brotherhood jurisdiction when committed in the country, wilderness, or unpopulated areas (hamlets with less than fifty residents were considered unpopulated).[29]

How the country would pay for these forces was not determined at Madrigal beyond a vague command that each local hermandad keep a "chest" from taxation with enough money to sustain its forces.[30] Specifics of finances and national organization were to be drawn up by Isabella's ministers and municipal representatives (who met at Madrigal from May 8 to May 13).[31] They were to report within thirty days for a second planning session wherein final details would be concluded. This second meeting was held on June 13 at Chigales, a small town near Valladolid, and presided over by Lope de Ribas, president of the Royal Council (the powerful governing body of Castile). Broad financial details were worked out and troop commitments set. Ferdinand and Isabella approved the plan in Valladolid on June 15.

The decisions of Madrigal and Chigales were combined and issued by the monarchs on that date as the first book of ordinances of the general brotherhood. These ordinances exhorted the kingdom to meet tax and troop commitments. To this end, each city, village, and hamlet was ordered to meet in council within eight days and take an oath on the cross and New Testament that the brotherhood would prevail. To coordinate policy, each province was to hold a meeting in its capital on July 1 for purposes of census, and all would later come together in a General Assembly, wherein progress would be evaluated and it would be determined which lands would have to be forced to enter the league.[33]

The Holy Brotherhood, as the league came to be called, did not differ in essentials from its predecessors.[34] Its ordinances were copied from previous books, duties of the rural police were in no way changed, and there is no mention of a militia. The Council, however, was already functioning behind scenes as an informal organizing committee. There is no suggestion that Isabella harbored plans for the league to continue after her succession was assured.

In friendly areas the fledgling organization proceeded with

dispatch. Provincial Assemblies met on July 1 to give formal acceptance to decisions already agreed upon. Reports from municipal records in Burgos show that in June its province had already agreed to provide troops.[35] To pay these costs taxes were to be laid on certain merchandise entering the city. A letter to this effect was dispatched on June 29 to the king, who thanked the city and

With preliminaries out of the way, the first General Assembly promised it significant favors.[36]

was then held at the end of July in Dueñas, a little town on a hill a few miles from Valladolid.[37]

Merely analyzing the legislation produced at meetings of the general hermandad misses much of the significance of the gatherings. Medieval men obscured the mean reality of politics and harsh laws with the glitter of steel and the drape of velvet. This craving for pageantry and pomp was fully appreciated by Ferdinand and Isabella. On the twenty-fifth day of July the royal couple moved in stately procession through the winding streets of Dueñas to the Church of Santa Maria de Dueñas to open the Assembly. The presence of the monarchy's retinue added to the pageantry of the occasion. The nobility were present, surrounded by their families, pages, and gentlemen. Both men and women wore rich velvets and silks; their long gloves were loaded with rings; collars and chains of gold adorned their necks. In the rear came members of the brotherhood from cities, villages, hamlets, and manors of the kingdoms, as well as representatives from the three estates thereof. Everyone attended: national and provincial delegates, captains, magistrates, alcaldes, attorneys, soldiers, and messengers. From the highest to the lowest order, vulgar display was the rule.[38]

The long procession wended its way toward the church of Santa Maria de Dueñas. The twelfth century church, although built in the Romanesque style, has pointed arches forecasting the advent of the Gothic. Thrones had been prepared within for the sovereigns, so that they might view the assembly from on high. Isabella was a woman of austere and chaste ways, but like her namesake Elizabeth I of England, she indulged herself in dress. On solemn occasions she appeared in robes of velvet, dazzling with jewels and precious stones, adorned like an Italian Madonna. She was twenty-six and in vigorous health. Her bright chestnut hair, almost red, was set off by a fair complexion. Floods of panegyrics have been written about her but portraits shock romantics by the homely, round face they reveal. It has been suggested that they do not reflect her good looks because her beauty was that of animation and will.

By her side was Ferdinand, king of Sicily, the title conferred upon him by his father as a wedding gift. His deeply tanned face, with its heavy sensuous lips and pensive eyes, contrasted strongly with his pale, tight-lipped bride. He was prematurely bald, muscular, and although heavy, well-proportioned. Ranged about the young couple were their advisors—Lope de Ribas, president of the Council, arrayed in the full splendor of a Spanish bishop; the duke of Villahermosa, supreme commander of the militia, reputedly the best soldier in Aragon; Juan de Ortega, also in bishop's robes; and Alfonso de Quintanilla, the soldier-book-keeper, driving force behind the brotherhood.

It would not be surprising if the splendor of the monarchs and great dignitaries awed the municipal representatives. Seated in rows before the thrones were town officials from Avila, Burgos, Medina, Olmeda, Palencia, Salamanca, Segovia, and Zamora.[39]

This assembly did not go smoothly. A revolt simmered among representatives whose cities would have to bear the financial burdens foreseen during the planning sessions. Isabella's chroniclers usually lay blame for all opposition to the brotherhood on malefactors or disgruntled nobility; however, this time Pulgar recorded an unusual event. From every side came objections to Ferdinand and Isabella's general brotherhood. Other schemes were suggested and then abandoned. When it appeared that no progress could be made, the delegates prepared to leave for their homes.

In the midst of the noisy disturbance Quintanilla rose and made an impassioned speech larded with religious and patriotic appeals, calling up visions of the brotherhood's great past, of the Moorish threat, and of the delusion of the king of Portugal. He frankly pointed out that they were not speaking of conquering foreign provinces but of conquest of their own land, their own villages, their own homes. Who could object to the cost of this work? Would not any man give half of his goods to assure that the other half were safe? To still doubts raised concerning the weakness of the previous leagues, he pointed to Ferdinand and Isabella's provision of a constitution as a token of authority they would lend to the new brotherhood. When he concluded, everyone, cavaliers, legists, townsmen, and rustics, agreed that the brotherhood would solve their problems and they would pay the costs and provide the men.[40]

Part of the reason the royal officials were able to overcome opposition to the general brotherhood was that it was presented as being a temporary institution (from August 15, 1476, to August 15, 1478).[41] The burden undertaken by the city men may not have seemed so onerous at the time because they were also assured that all classes were to contribute to the force's maintenance.[42]

An improved administrative structure for the brotherhood was proposed and accepted at Dueñas. The initial plan approved by the Cortes had called for conventional territorial divisions.[43] This was rejected at Dueñas in favor of subdividing the kingdomwide brotherhoods into several more or less equal provincial brotherhoods. Each province would hold elections in its municipalities for delegates to provincial assemblies.[44] Of course General Assemblies were still to be held once a year to bring officials together.[45] Thus at Dueñas the structure of Ferdinand and Isabella's brotherhood was completed. Members of the Council all appear, although the Council itself is not mentioned by name. It was agreed that one of the Council members, Ferdinand's brother Duke Alonso de Aragón, would direct a miniature army provided by the brotherhood for the queen's use.[46]

The decisions of Dueñas, known as the second book of ordinances, were approved by Ferdinand and Isabella on August 13.[47] Some items with disturbing consequences for the future were stated ambiguously in the final draft of the book. A decision was made to increase enormously the jurisdiction of the rural police beyond the limits set at the Cortes of Madrigal. A recently discovered, unedited copy of Pulgar's *Crónica de los Reyes Católicos* not published until 1943 brings to light five statutes that summarize the jurisdiction of the brotherhood agreed to at Dueñas. Two of these illustrate the wide use to which the monarchs intended to set their new forces. One statute gives the brotherhood jurisdiction for the first time over crimes committed in cities but only if the suspect flees (e.g., to another city or to a seignorial estate). His offense is to be punished by the brotherhood alcaldes as if it had been perpetrated in the countryside. The other statute records that the brotherhood was to punish anyone who went against justice or was disobedient.[48] This drastically expanded jurisdiction of the alcaldes (jurisdiction of almost any offense decided upon by the league wherever it took place) demonstrates the Council's intent to use the rural police as an adjunct to the brotherhood militia in reducing Castile to Isabella's rule. It meant a trampling over the rights of ordinary justice and a willingness on Isabella's part to authorize sweeping attacks upon Castilian freedom in the name of her new league.

One of the final observations regarding this Dueñas assembly is that only eight northern areas were represented.[49] The brotherhood was still little more than a formal alliance of Isabella's acknowledged supporters in the civil war. Pulgar's narrative demonstrates that even these friendly towns were unenthusiastic. Contrary to traditional assumptions, they held back from the very start and had to be pushed. Armed forces pledged were produced grudgingly. At a second session of the General Assembly held in August, again at Dueñas, the provinces of the cities of Leon, Zamora, and Salamanca were threatened with fines of 50,000 *maravedís* if their share of militiamen were not dispatched forthwith.[50]

By mid-1476, as the foregoing indicates, Ferdinand and Isabella had cemented control of most aspects of the league. The first two assembly meetings revealed the direction to be taken—incorporation of the whole kingdom under the Council's watchful eye. Where possible this was accomplished by persuasion; where necessary, by threats.

It was decreed at a meeting of the General Assembly in Toro

(December 12) that all cities of the realm join in a *hermandad universal* of Castile, Leon, Galicia, and Andalusia.[51] The scene of action shifted to the center of New Castile. A General Assembly called by Ferdinand and Isabella at San Miguel de Pino ordered sanctions against Ocaña, a large city near Toledo, if it did not join forthwith.[52] Isabella went herself to Ocaña where she was joined by her husband. Together they requested the municipal officials to enter into the Holy Brotherhood, eventually succeeding with the aid of some Sevillians.[53]

Next on the timetable were the Extremadurian cities near the Portuguese border. Before the start of this campaign, a General Assembly was held on March 1, 1477, at Dueñas, where a third book of ordinances was drawn up. It ordered that no community was to communicate with or pay debts to any "rebels" who had not yet joined the league. Once a city came into the league it would not be allowed to withdraw, under penalty of heavy fine. To assure that these mandates be carried out, the monarchs ordered that the national delegates (*diputados generales*) remain at the court. Ferdinand and Isabella decided in March 1477 to keep these men in continuous session even after the General Assemblies finished their business. The representatives became a Parliament of Delegates *(Diputación General)* under the wing of the Council president.[54] The Parliament was used to bring a continuity to policy enforcement that had been lacking. To snap the whip over the hermandades the Parliament elected an *ejecutor general* whom it sent into the provinces to see that its orders were carried out.[55]

In addition to this official, the crown also had its own magistrates in each provincial brotherhood to carry out royal mandates. This officer, the *juez ejecutor,* had the responsibility of overseeing the activities of the many city, village, and hamlet brotherhood officials under his jurisdiction.[56]

With the General Assembly completed, the anticipated military action took place in Extremadura against several small cities, including Trujillo. Isabella had several contingents of brotherhood troops in her army when she arrived at the gates of Trujillo in the middle of June. Trujillo's mayor, Pedro de Baeza, at first returned a hard answer to her demands for entrance, but as he was confronted by her troops and cannon he eventually delivered the city.[57]

A show of force quickly intimidates a small town but to gain the allegiance of aristocratic strongholds bloodlessly requires patience and diplomacy. The test that confronted Ferdinand and Isabella in the cities dominated by truculent Andalusian nobility required special finesse, for neither the duke of Medina Sidonia nor the young marques of Cadiz, though they had supported Isabella against Doña Juana, had any special love for the new queen.

The two nobles, however, were engaged in a long-standing blood feud and could not present a common front against the determined Isabella. Taking advantage of the rift, the monarchs concentrated their strategy upon bringing the duke around. During January 1477, while in residence at Ocaña, they decided to press the thriving commercial city of Seville, Medina Sidonia's stronghold, to join the league. Two Sevillians, Pedro del Algava and Juan Reyón, a brotherhood attorney, were commissioned on January 8 to undertake the task of convincing the city fathers that they must prove their loyalty to the sovereigns.[58] On the fifteenth Reyón was sent to the city with a letter summarizing the books of ordinance, calling upon the city fathers to join the league and threatening them with penalties and confiscation of goods if they did not comply.[59] Another letter on the same subject followed in five days entreating the city to look to the service of God and the universal good of the kingdom.[60]

When nothing availed, Palencia, who held the office of attorney general, was specially charged with bringing Seville into line.[61] On June 21 Isabella issued yet another letter directing Seville to form a brotherhood forthwith.[62] Palencia visited Ferdinand and Isabella at Medina del Campo and was given a copy of this last letter and a book of brotherhood laws that he was to present to the duke's representative, Francisco de Peña.[63] The duke continued to be uncooperative. Palencia and his two deputies, Algava and Reyón, decided to ignore the duke altogether and deal directly with the citizenry of Seville.

The city at which the three emissaries arrived still looked

Moorish. A retaining wall ran down from the Alcázar palace in the city's heart to a defense tower, the *Torre del Oro,* on the banks of the river Guadalquivir, and parts of the old mosque were still standing, although the main structure had been replaced by an enormous Gothic cathedral. Fruit trees in the Court of the Oranges embellished the cathedral as they had the mosque. Rising from the side of the cathedral was an old minaret, the high, slim Giralda Tower. In the narrow, winding streets around the cathedral, cool patios gave visitors some protection from the exhausting heat of summer.

The duke of Medina Sidonia was not in the city when the three emissaries arrived, and Palencia found the city council unwilling to make any decisions in his absence. In fact, the municipal leaders threatened dire results to anyone in the city who aided the militia. As Palencia tells the story, not stinting on his part in the exploits, they

> threatened Juan Reyón with the gallows, and Pedro del Algava with cutting his throat . . . The two deputies took refuge in the house of Pedro de Estuniga . . . but soon, because of cowardice, fear, or his natural vacillation, he appeared inclined to the opinions of the Duke, with the result that the deputies went to the Monastery of San Pablo. This left me to take part in the negotiations alone and I calmly resolved to confront the risk of meeting the irate Duke.[64]

Palencia was spared the danger because the six months of unremitting pressure on the city fathers at last produced the desired result. The duke had placed 400 loyal New Christians in the Alcázar fortress of Seville as a counter to Isabella's pressure. But the duke's advisors gradually became convinced of the futility of this opposition and upon the duke's return to the city confronted him with the reality that continued resistance could not be maintained. He had no reasonable alternative to offer against the advice of those present and the city agreed to join the league. With everything accomplished but the ceremony, Isabella made a grand entrance into Seville on the twenty-fifth of July, receiving the key to the Alcázar from Medina Sidonia's own hand. There she waited until the marques of Cadiz capitulated to her one evening in August. Palencia's labors had not been in vain.

The monarchs thus had cause for celebration when they attended the August 1477 Assembly at Burgos.[65] On the third of August the participants in this Assembly moved in procession through the great door of the white limestone cathedral, under its magnificent rose window.[66] Inside, in the little chapel of Saint Catharine, the Assembly sealed Isabella's triumph with liberal new grants of funds.[67]

The territorial expansion of the brotherhood was completed shortly after the capitulation of Seville with the surrender of all of Andalusia. The league then extended from the waters of the Atlantic to the Sierra Nevada of Granada. The Council, nevertheless, could not create a unity of purpose among all the cities in this vast expanse of territory. The founding municipalities had cooperated originally because their wartime alliance with Isabella yielded rewards, concessions, and the maintenance of privilege. Coercion had brought in neutral or hostile cities. The cement that held them all together at this point was only the threat of war, but as Juana's strength declined and the anticipated massive invasion by Portugal failed to materialize, unrest came out into the open.

The league was due to expire after May 15, 1478, and could not be renewed except by the organization itself.[68] Therefore a General Assembly had to be called promptly in the year and the crown ordered it to meet in early February in Seville. Important Council officials arrived but when the king could not come, the meeting was rescheduled for Madrid later in the month.[69] Ferdinand made sure that he attended this meeting, even abandoning suppression of an Andalusian uprising to do so.[70] The Madrid assembly was held in an atmosphere of hostility and apathy. Especially serious was the opposition in Andalusia, Toledo, and the cities on the Portuguese border.[71] Agitation was not limited to any one social group, but was widespread among all those who were asked to contribute to the brotherhood's upkeep.[72]

Opposition to renewing the brotherhood was neutralized only by royal claims that the militia was a military necessity.[73] Because Portugal was still a potent threat and fear of her a weapon easily manipulated, the crown was successful in having the brotherhood reauthorized before the expiration date. Its charter was, moreover, extended by an additional year, demonstrating rather well the developing agility of the monarchs in outstepping opposition. A royal edict issued at the assembly on March 7 informed the country of the new three-year promulgation and asked all subjects, Church, clergy, gentry, and *pecheros* (taxpayers) to meet assessments (contributions to start from August 15 of that year).[74]

Talk about ending the brotherhood cropped up again only a year later spurred on by rumors of impending peace with Portugal. Delegates to the General Assembly at Madrigal (June 7, 1479) pressed, on the basis of these rumors, to eliminate the league at once even though its charter had two years to run.[75] Although they had no success, sentiment for their point of view intensified when the long-awaited treaty of peace with Portugal was signed in September.[76] (Hostilities between the two countries were settled in Isabella's favor.)[77] Upon hearing of the treaty many cities summarily stopped payment of their quotas to the Council on the strength of the tradition that general brotherhoods dissolved after emergencies. This time the city fathers misjudged their freedom of action. The monarchs had reached a decision that the brotherhood was to be retained despite custom. Stiff letters were sent out to laggards by the Parliament of Delegates in December 1479 restating quotas, with a firm admonition that no excuses would be accepted for avoiding payment.[78] This was not enough. In the same month, at a General Assembly meeting in Toledo, the sovereigns issued a stern warning of their "deliberate and voluntary determination" that the league continue.[79] All captains, alcaldes, magistrates, and deputies were ordered to punish any delinquents, either individuals or city corporations. So that no one could pretend ignorance of this decree, it was published in every marketplace and public site.[80]

A general tightening-up followed throughout the realm. Lists were published in January 1480 of municipalities that had not yet entered the league.[81] Brotherhood majordomos were ordered to put pressure on their communities and strong letters were sent out to cities that had not yet paid their quotas.[82] Firmness brought the desired result—the brotherhood would continue.

It is remarkable that despite increasing urban opposition the monarchs were able to gain their way. One is led to conclude that the fifteenth century Castilian city was weaker than has yet been suspected. As long as rival noble factions were available to challenge a reigning monarch, the urban class maintained some measure of independence; but faced with Ferdinand and Isabella's cunning in satisfying the nobility, isolated cities proved impotent.

3

The Brotherhood and the Castilian Municipalities, 1480-1498

THE YEAR 1480 sealed Ferdinand and Isabella's victory over the cities. At the annual General Assembly in Madrid in August 1480 a new book of ordinances, the fourth, was issued that revealed a new balance between monarchy and municipality. From the first to the last clause, its text was peppered with royal commands regarding *our powers, our mandates, our orders,* and *our officials.*[1] Cities no longer dared repeat the language of the second book of ordinances (1476). Then they had insisted that the lifetime of the league be strictly limited to one term and after that period no one was obligated to pay taxes "even if demanded to do so by the King and Queen, or the Council."[2] The 1480 book offers instead evidence of Ferdinand and Isabella's confidence: the General Assembly voted a new extension (1481 to 1483) a full year before the old term expired; the militia was expanded and reorganized; and the brotherhoods of Andalusia and Galicia were to raise funds for a navy.[3]

But there were still critics to mollify. The ordinances of 1480 were both a show of dominion and an acquiescence to criticism. Defects of the brotherhood were to be remedied: overtaxing of the cities was to cease; officers and men of the militia were to stop sequestering provender; and alcaldes were prohibited from making a show of riches. Measures were also taken to clear up legal tangles. The monarchs admitted the need to clarify the laws to eliminate ambiguity and prolixity. To this end an eminent legist, Gonzalo Gonzalez de Illescas, judge of the Royal *Audiencia*, was appointed to the Council in the position of general advocate. He was to reside with the Parliament of Delegates to give them the benefit of his advice.

These minor concessions were all that the critics obtained from the queen in 1480. For her few promises she gained a great deal in the following years. Taxes began to mount steadily as she moved to exploit her domination of the league. Even the proposed judicial reform proved hollow, and it is clear that she had no intention of inhibiting the ruthless justice of the rural police. To avoid stalling the machine while repairs were being considered, the 1480 book ordered the alcaldes not to let doubts over jurisdiction hold them up. Once proceedings commenced, alcaldes were not to let appeal, however high the court, impede their activities.[4] In sum, this is further evidence of urban political weakness. There is no pretense in the 1480 book that the crown and the cities were on an equal footing. The pleas of the urban classes were disregarded. Eventually defects in the league were to be corrected, but change was to come as a boon from the throne in its own good time.

In the years after 1480 renewals of the life of the brotherhood were given by General Assemblies almost automatically under pressure of a new war. The Council effectively became a semipermanent part of the government during the Granada War. From 1483 to 1491 the prime work of the Council was to prosecute this struggle. Naturally the militia expanded during these years, but there were also important domestic consequences of the war. Initial skirmishes with the Moors in 1482 showed that Castile was unable to win a quick victory. Ferdinand and Isabella's government had to find immediate means to increase the military strength of the kingdom. The Holy Brotherhood would have to carry a heavier load.

In March 1483 an extremely stormy session of the Burgos Provincial Assembly ensued when the monarchs revealed the extent of their demands: 17,000 beasts of burden and 8,000 men for drovers. The delegates assailed the arbitrary increases, the harsh methods of collection, and even the tax officials, this despite the chairing of the meeting by Quintanilla. Eventually the delegates were quieted down and convinced to vote their share of the special levy.[5] The monarchs were not yet finished. At the General Assembly, held in November 1483 at Miranda de Ebro, a special grant of ten million maravedís was voted for the war. The third extension of the life of the league was approved as well (from August 15, 1484, to August 15, 1487).[6]

When Ferdinand and Isabella came to the next General Assembly (at Orgaz, in November 1484) for another contribution, they were prepared with a plan that eased their future path. After the Assembly agreed to a ten and one-half million maravedís extraordinary grant, the queen resolved to show her satisfaction with their loyalty by contributing twelve million from her own purse to pay in full for the grant and even cutting back on the ordinary quota.[7] The monarchs recognized the calming effects of propaganda. They were well aware that Assembly representatives should be wooed, despite the underlying powerlessness of the cities to resist the increasing taxes. The generosity of 1484 was but a prelude to vast new financial demands made the following year.

Generally speaking, taxes were nearly doubled by the fiscal settlement of 1485. This time the crown bought acquiescence from the cities with extensive reform of legal procedures. At the General Assembly, which opened in 1485 at Torrelaguna, an ancient walled town near Madrid, the king and queen coupled their request for funds with a guarantee that intrusion into local rights by the brotherhood would be halted. The monarchs tried to satisfy the municipal representatives by revoking the vast and conflicting body of ordinances and decrees that had built up.[8]

A fresh legal start was made by the Ordinances of Torrelaguna.[9] A major step was taken at Torrelaguna to answer the cities' continuing plaint that alcaldes meddled in all phases of justice. Jurisdiction of brotherhood police was completely reshaped and judges' statutes were made very detailed and specific.

To give but one example, the first clause of the new statutes dealt with robbery or damage to goods and rape of women who were not prostitutes. Jurisdiction of these crimes fell to the brotherhood only when they took place in the wilderness or in unpopulated areas. If these crimes were committed in populated sites, brotherhood alcaldes were to try the cases only if the malefactors later fled to the countryside with the goods or the woman. Other statutes treated with equal explicitness the brotherhood's role in crimes involving highwaymen, private jails, arson, attacks upon brotherhood officials, and protection of officers during General Assemblies. Only these crimes were specified for brotherhood jurisdiction.[10]

A major attempt was made to force alcaldes into town judicial systems. They were ordered to act in reciprocity with ordinary justice and to remit cases not within their jurisdiction. Moreover, the rights of ordinary justice were finally listed in the brotherhood's books. Special attention was also given to appeal. Pleas could now be made from decisions of justices of the brotherhood to superior judges having ordinary jurisdiction.[11]

Why were these reforms made at this time? In addition to the already suggested aim of easing the way for new taxes, there is a strong aura of administrative convenience about the 1485 book. One consequence of the prolongation of the Granada struggle was that Royal Council members had to give increasing attention to the war, a situation common to governments involved in lengthy conflicts. As a consequence it became necessary in Castile to make the smooth operation of the brotherhood police less dependent upon constant Council review and interference. This move toward judicial reform, although belated, was in harmony with Ferdinand and Isabella's ideal that royal justice should be uniform and evenhanded toward all subjects.

Despite these legal reforms, cities still had cause for dissatisfaction. All problems of jurisdiction were not solved, and the brotherhoods had not been humbled. They retained for a time such rights as the ability of the brotherhood jailor of Seville to keep out unwanted visitors to his cells. Not until after 1486, after vigorous protests by residents, did the queen insist that the jailor allow municipal delegations to visit cells to see who was incarcerated and upon what charge.[12] The Council still occasionally had to settle jurisdictional disputes. In 1486 it intervened to reprove some alcaldes for disturbing a marshal in his jurisdiction,[13] and in 1487 it reprimanded other alcaldes for meddling in a provincial governor's realm.[14] Alcaldes were also called to task by the Council in disputes involving the protests of the wealthy or of powerful institutions. For example, in 1491, the monarchs sent an emissary to Cordova to investigate a complaint from an agent of the Inquisition that he was injured by officials of that city's brotherhood on the pretext that he retained a criminal in his lodgings.[15]

Despite reprimands, the brotherhoods continued to bask in the glow of their queen's affection, as they would until she no longer needed their cooperation to fight her wars. The Council was vigilant in protecting brothers from arbitrary acts of outside authority. In 1489 two such attempts were reviewed at court. Municipal records were investigated by the Council in the case of a brotherhood archer who was imprisoned by a corregidor (a powerful crown representative in cities).[16] In another case an ordinary alcalde was ordered to present himself at court after he banished a brotherhood alcalde from his city.[17] When necessary, the Council

Hermandad infantrymen in crusader dress during the Granada War

prevented irate city governments from seizing goods of hermandad officials. The city of Burgos, for example, was ordered in 1488 to return to the wives of two alcaldes personal goods sequestered when their husbands were jailed.[18]

The queen's continuing partiality towards the brotherhood was an irritant to the cities. But it was only a minor cause of friction compared to frustration over rising taxation. The struggle with the kingdom of Granada dragged on year after year with ever increasing assessments. Foremost among dissenters was initially cooperative Burgos, which soon bridled at the endless expense.[19] This was an important defection because the city was a vital economic center. Burgos was one of the principal trading communities of Europe, and its famous fair of Medina del Campo brought merchants from everywhere to bargain for fine wool, cloth, silk, and jewelry. Wealth pouring into Burgos made it an impressive metropolis with magnificent buildings and markets, fine bridges across the river Arlanzón, numerous churches, and a grand cathedral.

Burgos was governed by a salaried municipal corporation of from four to seven alcaldes and up to sixteen aldermen (regidores). Some of these offices were filled by the crown, the rest by the city. The corporation sat throughout the week, and all officers had equal power. There was no president but a chief scribe who could not vote but could initiate actions and present matters for deliberation. This was rule by a tight oligarchy. The principal officials held their offices for life and with crown permission passed them on to their children.[20]

Records of the corporation show that city fathers took a firm position in 1483 that they did not need the brotherhood league to govern or defend Burgos, and they refused to pay anything toward the next quota. The Council retaliated by threatening Burgos with severe penalties, including sequestering of goods and loss of commercial privileges. Although the city corporation capitulated, it swore that when the new extension lapsed it would quit itself of all obligation to the brotherhood.[21] To show their strength of will they ignored payment of extraordinary taxes voted at the General Assembly of Orgaz (November 1484) for the Granada War, saying that the regular quota for 1485 was sufficient.[22]

The Council was outraged when the city continued on its independent way. General administrators Quintanilla and Ortega dispatched a blistering letter to the Burgos corporation that was read aloud in the session of December 28, 1486. They castigated the city fathers for instructing their representative, Diego González del Castillo, to speak out against continuing the league at the General Assembly of Tordesillas (November 1486) in the face of obvious war needs. Furthermore, nonpayment of the new quota was setting a bad example for surrounding areas, an act which the monarchs regarded with hostility. The general administrators threatened heavy penalties, including the impounding of a sum equal to the unpaid subsidy.[23] Under this pressure the city gave in again and paid for the new term.

Burgos was not alone in its obstructionism, although its case is most fully documented. Seville offered passive opposition to brotherhood taxation in 1480 and 1482.[24] Toledo also deliberately failed to meet its obligations on time, the area, Benito Ruano informs us, in which the interests of the city and the Reyes Católicos most conflicted.[25] Burgos, Seville, and Toledo were major cities, on a par with the greatest in Europe. Yet their protest and obstruction had remarkably little effect on Council policy. They were cowed by mere threats of economic reprisals. Castilian cities' possibilities of retaliation appear absurdly limited, their inability to coordinate policy indicative of the causes for their impotence.

After the great Christian victory at Granada the Council's activities must have fallen off sharply. The militia never again saw combat and after 1492 only the regular contribution had to be collected. Documentation becomes limited at this point and it is even difficult to determine times and places of General Assemblies.[26] One was held in October 1491 [27] and another before May of 1492.[28] The third postwar General Assembly met at Soria on July 7, 1493, and voted a sixth extension of the life of the league

(August 15, 1493, to August 15, 1496).[29] There may have been an assembly in 1494,[30] but the last one of which mention is found was held at Santa Maria del Campo in June 1495, where another extension was voted.[31]

Despite this prolongation, urban opposition to the Santa Hermandad reemerged with the end of the Granada War. In 1494 the brotherhood council of the province of Seville had to complain to the monarchs that the city of Seville was preventing it from collecting taxes and fulfilling the laws. Ferdinand and Isabella promised a royal visitation to invigorate taxation, but in the same letter assuaged the city fathers by issuing the following reforms to the brotherhood of Seville: to prevent excessive fines, the judgments levied by alcaldes were to be set by the city's scribe (who set ordinary exchequer fines); alcaldes were not to usurp rights of pardon falling to ordinary justice; and the jailor of the brotherhood was ordered to cease interference in the rights of the warden of the city prison.[32]

Later in the year the monarchs had further trouble with the city. Seville deprived Alonso de las Cuevas of the office of brotherhood scribe, charging that he had committed excesses causing aggravations and damages. The case was brought before the Council by Pedro Sanchez de Arbolancha, an official of the crown in Seville. The Council ruled that the scribe was dispoiled of possession of his office, and on August 30, 1494, ordered that he be restored to office.[33]

The Council might well have continued on indefinitely. The decision to keep or disband the league lay by this time squarely in the monarch's hands. The main value of the Council to the queen was in its control of the troops; thus when the militia became obsolete the council was no longer necessary. Definite legislative steps led to the dissolution of the militia and the disbandment of the Council.

At the General Assembly of 1495 the monarchs proposed that plans be laid to eliminate taxation for the national organization.[34] In order to implement this change a new book of ordinances, the first in a decade, was issued from Cordova on July 7, 1496. These laws restate clauses of the 1485 Ordinances of Tordesillas dealing with the election, duties, and discipline of alcaldes and archers, but are silent concerning the militia, the Council, and assemblies.[35] After this point the monarchs moved rapidly to complete their plans. In 1497 the brotherhood militia was deactivated, although no change was made in taxation levels.[36] Then, without any warning, on July 29, 1498, Isabella issued a decree from Zaragoza officially lifting the contribution for the defunct militia and unexpectedly dismantling the entire superstructure of the Council, leaving only the skeletal remains of the local police forces. Suddenly, by royal fiat, she had wiped out a league of cities that had existed for twenty-two years.

Her action made excellent sense to the generation grown up since 1476. The decree devoted space to a history of her brotherhood, explaining that it was created to eliminate anarchy and then kept to defeat the Moors. The queen long regretted the heavy contributions paid by her subjects, and with peace and tranquility at last restored she was freeing them from taxes and vexation.[37]

There were a few reservations to the queen's magnanimous act. A reference was made to the threat of war with the king of France, an oblique way of warning her subjects of new taxes they would be called upon to pay for a royal army. In addition, the queen made no move to eliminate the rural police. Ordinances of 1485 were kept in force to provide for justice, security and safety on the roads; thus taxation for archers and alcaldes would continue.[38]

Isabella's preservation of the hermandades demonstrates the deep roots that this institution had in the soil of Castilian municipal life. The brotherhoods are an illuminating example of the continuity of Spanish tradition, passing unscathed through a temporary absorption in Ferdinand and Isabella's Santa Hermandad and continuing on into the modern world, still patrolling highways as they had centuries before.

Hermandad archer carrying crossbow (from 1746 book of laws of the Holy Brotherhood).

4

The Brotherhood and the Castilian Aristocracy

NOWHERE in fifteenth-century Western Europe were lords prouder and more powerful, nowhere towns weaker and fewer than in Castile, according to the respected authority, Garrett Mattingly.[1] Ferdinand and Isabella were realists willing to make accommodations when it suited their purpose. Monarchs who wished to increase their political power in this era would have to be willing to give economic favors and some important offices to nobility. Indeed, there was no other real option. Towns could not provide alternative support because they were no longer strong or united.

Also, towns were often dominated by the lords. This fact is supported by the research of Benito Ruano[2] and Tarsicio de Azcona.[3] Benito Ruano points out that in fifteenth century Toledo landowning nobility had so firmly entrenched itself that the Ayalas and other great families were virtual chieftains. They dominated so many municipal offices that residents obeyed their commands, even if it meant rebellion against the crown. Father Azcona gives us examples of cities in Andalusia completely dominated by aristocrats: Seville (duke of Medina Sidonia); Trujillo (marques of Villena); Almora (duke of Valencia); Carmona (count of Urueña); Cordova (alternating factions of Alvaro de Aguilar and Diego Fernández de Córdoba, count of Cabra).[4]

The aristocracy's demonstrable strength influenced the way Ferdinand and Isabella dealt with them, of course, but there is another factor that colored relations with their nobility. It was, simply put, a belief in the rightness of the established order. Ferdinand and Isabella's overall social views could best be described as "traditionalist" and "constitutional." Each estate was entitled to its rights so long as these rights did not conflict with the full exercise of a royal authority limited by the fundamental laws and by God.[5]

Hence, although Ferdinand and Isabella made full use of their cunning and powers to achieve internal order and complete the Reconquest, it would not have occurred to them to reshuffle the estates to do so. The functions of nobility, clergy, and multitude were clear and unalterable. The function of the Third Estate was to pay its taxes quietly, and the crown expected nothing more. Vicens Vives points out that all the burghers received from the monarchs was order and a relatively prosperous economy.[6] But even this was hardly a matter of policy as economic considerations always ran a poor third to the demands of war or religion. For example, two commercially important groups, the New Christians and the Jews, were persecuted despite violent objections from the governing corporations of Barcelona, Seville, Toledo, Valencia, and Zaragoza, which correctly foresaw a drain of capital out of Castile to the rest of Europe.[7]

On the other hand, the privilege of nobility was to lead society and much attention was paid to their status. The aristocracy was not trampled upon. Vicens Vives buttresses the argument of Isabella's partiality toward them with concrete proof He examines the distributions of favors during the reign and calls attention to a discovery that the nobility continued to tighten its grip on Castilian land. This corrects a misleading impression that the Cortes of 1480 had significant results when it demanded that royal lands usurped by grandees be returned. Only a very small percentage of thefts ever found their way back to the crown.[8] Even this insignificant loss was more than made up to the grandees by the gain of the lands of Granada.[9]

The best available estimates of real estate owned by the high nobility show that two to three percent of the population had ninety-seven to ninety-eight percent of the land and over one half of this was in the hands of a few great families.[10] Houses like Velasco, Enríques, Toledo, Mendoza, Guzmán, Pacheco, and Córdoba expanded their territorial holdings and increased their enormous wealth. Giving further patronage to these clans was natural. It was one of the only ways to win their powerful support.

So long as the nobility did not usurp royal privileges or engage in private warfare, Isabella gave to them everything that tradition sanctioned. They retained immunity from taxation, from torture, and from imprisonment for debt.[11] Despite the well-known reforms of 1480 in the Royal Council, which appear to signify the triumph of the university-trained legist, low-born advisors obtained only minor government offices. The plums still fell to the great nobility as viceroyalties, governorships, and most higher army posts.[12]

Given this enormous power of the great lords, the question arises as to why some cooperated at first in the establishment of the brotherhood. It is a safe generalization that they normally opposed innovation which increased the power of the crown. But exceptions would have to be made in times of crisis. Thus in 1468, when King Henry's throne appeared lost, a group of his noble supporters were willing to sign a formal pact of union with a brotherhood league.[13] Similarly, the emergency precipitated in 1475 by an impending Portuguese invasion caused Isabella's supporters to agree to a new brotherhood.[14]

But as the Portuguese threat waned, the continuing expansion of the Holy Brotherhood, with its attendant strengthening of the monarch's armed might, rekindled resentment. The high estates had anticipated a quick end to the brotherhood when Isabella was firmly seated upon the throne. The grandees and the great clergy were set against allowing the league to continue, but individual complaints could not persuade the monarchs to bring it to an end. Matters finally came to a boil in 1477 at Cabena when the high nobility held a stormy meeting to protest Isabella's policies, including her support of the brotherhood.[15] Under the leadership of Hurtado de Mendoza, duke of the Infantado, a petition was prepared for presentation to the queen charging that, "The newly established Brotherhood must be abolished. It is a burden on the people and an abomination to the great. . . ."[16] But Isabella would not heed their complaints.[17] Even feeling as she did about the value and importance of her grandees, she insisted that she would keep her militia. This was a matter of royal power that involved her prerogatives.

Despite the understandable rebuff she gave to the grandees' complaints, it is not simple to evaluate why they did not continue to press her further. I find no suggestion that concessions were made to mute the complaints. Perhaps the grandees were not sufficiently united to impose their will. The common front that they maintained in forbidding their own territories to enter the league did not last long. A major breakthrough for the crown was provided by the enormously wealthy northern landowner and great lord of Old Castile, the count of Haro, one of Isabella's earliest supporters. Not only did he cause all of his lands to enter the league by 1477, but he also exhorted his vassals to imitate his example.[18] He alone among the grandees is specifically mentioned in the chronicles as an active supporter of Isabella's plan. There is no reason to doubt Pulgar's evaluation that Haro's assistance was motivated by friendship and loyalty. Later, following Haro's example, the nobility of the kingdoms of Toledo, Andalusia, Extremadura, and Murcia fell into line.[19] A measure of the Council's eventual success in incorporating all seignorial territories of the kingdom into the league can be demonstrated in tax assessment sheets. One such document for 1496 in the Municipal Archives of Seville, which lists forty-six cities and villages, includes lands of the duke of Medina Sidonia, the duke of Arcos, and the countess of Molares.[20]

Despite Isabella's defiance of her grandees to bring about acceptance for her brotherhood, there was an absence of severity on her part with the nobility once the league was established. The value the queen placed upon a patent of nobility makes one hesitant in assuming that she ever intended the brotherhood to be used to depress the grandees' status.

In light of the crown's respect for its aristocracy, it is not unnatural that when important appointments had to be made for the brotherhood they went to this estate. The Council members and high provincial officials were drawn from its ranks. While it is not as easy to identify the social level of all of the lower officials, it is known that of every two alcaldes in each district one had to be a knight (*caballero*) of second grade nobility (*escudero*) and one was a city dweller and taxpayer.[21] Although the men shared equal responsibilities, the knight's salary was much higher. In Seville, for example, a knight received 20,000 maravedís per year, while his burgher associate was paid only 10,000.[22]

It is therefore not surprising to discover that this league did not set about overturning longstanding aristocratic rights. Grandees retained their personal exemptions from taxation, and residents of seignorial territory paid fewer brotherhood taxes than free city dwellers (subject peasants contributed to low lump-sum quotas, while townsmen were individually assessed the full rate per household).[23]

Even when Isabella tried a famous experiment, requesting universal taxation to share the burden of the brotherhood, the end result was a victory for traditional rights. At the first General Assembly the Council was presented as an institution for the national good and one therefore that all estates should help finance.[24] A special plea on religious grounds was also made to clerics and nobles that the brotherhood was needed not only for the pacification of the country but for a holy war against Granada.[25] Isabella could not easily carry out her intentions of equitable taxation in the face of ancient privilege. Soon after the *pecheros* (taxpayers) had agreed to contribute their share, the *hidalgos* (lower nobility) petitioned the crown to recognize their traditional personal exemption from taxes. They supplicated the queen to remember the burdens they already bore or had borne: their fathers had served against the Moors; they themselves were serving in the present civil war, prepared to die in the queen's service.[26] The monarch retreated and confirmed the right of the gentry not to contribute to the brotherhood ". . . all the years that it lasted."[27] This exemption was extended as well to female gentry on November 24, 1476.[28] Ferdinand and Isabella's tax policy shows all the marks of experimentation. When their initial attempt at universal taxation was rebuffed, the monarchs retreated. It was easier to cooperate with the nobles than to be in constant conflict with them. Also, their help was needed for the very process of ruling because the royal bureaucracy was simply too small to govern the country without their cooperation.

Ferdinand and Isabella were more successful in taxing the clergy, but only after a time. At first the church contributed no more to the brotherhood than a mite for the upkeep of bridges and buildings.[29] Despite repeated requests from the monarchs to the papacy, the clergy also retained their personal exemptions.[30] After years of vacillation by the crown, the total exemption of clerics and friars (and hidalgos) was specified in the 1485 reformed book of ordinances.[31] Only two years later, however, the clergy suffered a lasting reversal when a new pope, Innocent VIII, was persuaded to issue a bull obligating them at last to contribute to the brotherhood quota.[32]

During the years in which the crown tried to persuade the higher orders to agree to some taxation, the hard-pressed cities also looked to tap this wealth, but monarchs ware careful to protect their important subjects from municipal levies. When excise taxes for the brotherhood were laid by cities on goods destined for use by "exempted persons," royal prestige backed up protest petitions filed by clergy and nobility.[33] The monarchs did not wish to antagonize their aristocracy merely to aid townsmen in fulfilling quotas.

Although the acceptance of the league throughout the kingdom was indeed a triumph for royal prerogative, on the other hand little was lost by the aristocracy. The Council exerted its power unevenly, hardly disturbing the nobility while the Third Estate in free cities bore a heavy burden. The point is often raised that the brotherhood was used militarily and judicially by the crown against irresponsible grandees who were a cause of Castile's anarchy.[34] Palencia and Pulgar give evidence for military repression of overly powerful subjects. Upon examination of their texts, however, it is clear that campaigns undertaken by brotherhood troops against "tyrant fortresses" were in reality aiming at destruction of partisans of Princess Juana.[35] There is no reason to believe Isabella was motivated to expend her resources in these undertakings by an altruistic love of justice.

Another source for the view that the brotherhood was primarily intended as a tool for the reduction of highborn troublemakers is found in the books of ordinances. In 1477 brotherhood alcaldes were allowed for the first time to take actions against distinguished persons who would ordinarily have been exempted from their jurisdiction.[36] But this law of 1477 was only the codification of an emergency measure, not repeated in later books, and one the alcaldes seem to have made little use of except against partisans of the lost cause. The one name we come upon principally in the National Archives in Simancas is that of the count of Aguilar, one of Juana's chief allies. In 1476 the alcaldes of Soria moved against Aguilar's land for his crime of "smuggling" 3,000 sheep.[37] The only other significant documents we find deal with counteractions of the brotherhood after grandees interfered with tax collection. When in 1480 the duke of Medina Sidonia did not allow taxes to be paid by his subject lands, a severely worded threat was issued by the Parliament of Delegates.[38] Several other cases of similar offenses on a lesser scale were also discovered.[39]

Little else involving the brotherhood courts in the prosecution of high or low nobility was found, although without doubt further research may turn up more evidence. It appears likely, however, that offenses of the grandees and their retainers were settled by negotiation and conciliation when possible rather than by a constant threat of physical retribution. The royal army, even one including a few thousand brotherhood militia troops, was hardly enough to deter the grandees. The more powerful noble families could raise troops far in excess of anything available to the crown.

It is well known that the great bulk of armed men mustered for Granada at the start of the war arrived under the personal command of the lords. The Renaissance monarchy had to gain its way through prestige, conciliation, patronage, and constant personal contact whenever possible. It is absurd to hold that the great nobility could have been frightened into submission by the puny forces of the brotherhood.

My emphasis on the modest nature of the brotherhood's actions against the high aristocracy does not preclude mentioning the assistance that it gave Isabella in regaining some lost prerogatives. During the Council's first two years some permanent inroads were made into the strongholds of the grandees. Alcaldes were given the right, in 1476, to enter estates with four or five archers to search for criminals.[40] In addition, private prisons for debtors were ordered abolished in 1477. This prohibition was extended in 1485 to all private jailings except where the aim was only to hold a prisoner until he could be turned over to ordinary justice.[41] The intent of these laws was to give the crown some control over manorial justice, but analysis of the actual impact of these incursions into seignorial privilege will require intensive research into private archives. Until this research is done, we will not know how often an alcalde dared to take action against a defiant grandee.

5

The Council Chain of Command

GOVERNMENT remained personal in the reign of Ferdinand and Isabella. When they created a Council for the brotherhood they staffed this body with trustworthy royal officers. Loyalty had to make up for a lack of bureaucratic safeguards against temptations to misuse the military power of the hermandades. As may be seen in the listing of officers, the functions these officials discharged were similar to their more important duties on the powerful Royal Council of Castile, which ruled the land in the queen's name.

President of the Council and of the Parliament of Delegates
> 1476   Don Lope de Ribas, bishop of Cartagena, president of the Royal Council (died 1479)

> 1480   Don Alfonso de Burgos, bishop of Cordova, Cuenca, queen's confessor

Supreme Commander of the Troops
> Don Alonso de Aragón, duke of Villahermosa (brother of Ferdinand)

Chief Administrators and Universal Delegates
> Don Alfonso de Quintanilla, chief royal auditor, and his as-

sistant, Don Juan de Ortega, bishop of Almeria, queen's sacristan

Attorney General
Alonso de Palencia, member of the Royal Council, historian

Advocate General
Don Gonzalo Sanchez de Illescas, judge of the Audiencia, advocate of the Royal Council (appointed 1480)

Constable of Castile
Don Pedro Fernandez de Velasco (joined during the Granada War)

Although the queen presented her selections for the Santa Hermandad Council to General Assemblies and to the Cortes merely for their approval, in theory at least the Council's powers derived from the consent of the urban communities. Council members were given the following duties by the league: (1) presiding over the assemblies and the Parliament of Delegates; (2) ascertaining that taxes be paid, collected, and audited; (3) raising, maintaining, and directing militia troops; (4) disciplining alcaldes and police; and (5) judging appeals and smoothing conflicts in jurisdictions. To carry out these functions the seven member Council made use of the services of a small administrative group of legists, accountants, and tax experts: the overseers of the brotherhood, the administrative staff, and the chief treasurers and receivers. The overseers of the brotherhood were Juan Diaz de Alcocer, chief auditor of accounts; Pedro Diaz de la Torre, attorney general of the Royal Council; and Dr. Rodrigo Maldonado de Talavera. The administrative staff was composed of Don Juan de Molina, head scribe and secretary to Alonso de Aragón; his assistants in 1476, Diego López, Pedro Daza, and Francisco Medina; and Antonio Rodríguez de Lillo, advocate of the Royal Council. The chief treasurers and chief receivers were (1476) Pedro Gonzalez de Madrid, chief treasurer of Seville; (1488) Abraham Seneor, former chief farmer of royal revenue, and Rabbi

Meir Melamed, his successor; (1490) Louis de Santagel, chief treasurer of Aragon, and Francisco Pinelo, magistrate of Seville; (1494) Alonso Gutierres, royal treasurer and magistrate of Toledo, and Fernando de Villareal.

Despite the smooth flow of titles and duties assembled here for study, governance of the brotherhood was by no means tidy in practice. The many striking successes of Ferdinand and Isabella's reign have been so well treated in older histories that we may confine ourselves to an examination of some failures and halfway measures that also characterize their government. As J. H. Elliot observes in *Imperial Spain*: "If the introduction of administrative uniformity and centralization of power in the monarch's hands were the essential features of the Renaissance State, the Spain of Ferdinand and Isabella would hardly seem to qualify."[2]

The brotherhood Council itself was not highly structured. On the contrary, chancellery scribes did not even have a fixed formula for the name of the body. The monarchs refer to it as *nuestro concejo de las cosas de la Hermandad*,[3] *nuestro concejo que entienden en la cosas de la Hermandad*,[4] and other variants, until late in the Granada War, when reference is first found to the *concejo de la Hermandad*.[5] Scribes who were assigned to brotherhood business did not always mention the Council in their letters. Officials of the brotherhood felt free to issue orders without identifying their Council office, or without so much as mentioning the Council. This oversight is understandable in view of the fact that members of the brotherhood Council were generally members of some more important body. The scribes would naturally tend to use the more awesome title.

Besides, most of the Council's work was routine. We find a heavy volume of correspondence each year, but upon examination much of this labor involved reviewing complaints directed to the queen by the brotherhood officials, government functionaries, and aggrieved individuals. Royal orders were then sent out in her name, as requested. The Council served, as well, as a mere clearing house for dissemination of information and instruction.[6] Day-to-day supervision of brotherhood business could therefore be conducted by a few officials. Indeed, most of the work was in the hands of only two men, the general administrators and universal delegates, Alfonso de Quintanilla and his assistant Juan de Ortega. Quintanilla was the driving force behind the Council through its twenty-two years. His name appears on many Council letters on such varied subjects as taxes, troop allocation, discipline, or justice.

Quintanilla was a competent official but his control over the brotherhood fell far short of being total. Elements in the chain of command, theoretically subordinate, still retained independence. Starting with the General Assemblies, we find that the crown nominated, with local approval, only one of the two delegates sent by each province. The other delegate was elected by, and received his orders from, the provincial brotherhood.[7] Thus at the first level below the Council in the command pyramid, control comes not from above, but from below. A few weeks prior to the General Assembly meeting each province held its own convention (*junta provincial*).[8] It was vital that the Council control these assemblies to insure that the instructions they drew up for their representatives agreed with crown policy. Of course, at times the instructions given at these provincial assemblies to their General Assembly delegates were hostile to the sovereigns. Until well into the Granada War, instructions often called for the abolition of the Council. Even in later years an occasional delegate was ordered by his province or city to offer resistance to the monarch's plans.[9] Also, no higher official, either from the Council or from the Parliament of Delegates, had a right to appoint the municipal officials they supervised. Each jurisdiction thus elected its own alcaldes.[10]

Each sizable municipality had its own corporation (*cabildo*) for its brotherhood. A corporation consisted of several elected officials (*regidores* and *jurados*) who selected one of their own number as the *mayor* or majordomo. The workhorses of the brotherhood, the alcaldes and the constables, were answerable to him. Ultimate control of the brotherhood league lay within these corporations, with officials who could neither be appointed nor removed by the crown.

This basic defect in Council control over the league derives from the nature of Isabella's expediency. Rather than create a new institution she chose to adapt an old one to her needs. Brotherhood leagues had traditions that had to be respected. One of these, to give an extended example, was that brotherhood funds did not belong to the crown. Each provincial and municipal brotherhood had its own independent treasury. The national funds of the general brotherhoods could not (in theory at least) be touched by the monarchs. In 1480 when Ferdinand and Isabella moved to dip into the Council's treasury for their own needs, the Cortes of Toledo presented a memorial questioning whether the sovereigns had obtained a papal brief (necessary because of the sacred privileges of the Holy Brotherhood) before disposing of any money.[11] In 1492 this treasury was still intact and was indeed the only available money that Isabella could suggest be lent to finance Columbus's first voyage.[12] The loan, for it was not a royal gift, was paid back in full to the brotherhood.[13]

Finally, the most glaring failure of Ferdinand and Isabella's program for the hermandades derived from the regional separatism of their kingdoms, which they never succeeded in eradicating. A long-range perspective of Spanish history prior to Ferdinand and Isabella shows a constant enlargement and absorption of petty kingdoms into unified states, exemplified by the lasting merger of Castile with Leon in 1230. Ferdinand and Isabella flew in the face of this tradition. Despite their willingness to operate a joint kingship, the separate states of Castile and Aragon were maintained. Many political and economic areas where a true union could have been advanced were neglected. Castile alone shared in the spoils of Granada and the benefits of the New World. In return, Aragon was left completely to its own laws and customs. The fragile nature of Ferdinand and Isabella's "personal union" was revealed by its total collapse upon Isabella's death.[14]

Unification of the brotherhoods in all the realms was never achieved. The council studied in this book operated only in Castile, Leon, Galicia, and Andalusia. The Basque provinces of

Alava and Guipuzcoa were left to go their separate ways.[15] The independent status of this Basque league was confirmed on January 15, 1488, in a royal letter issued from Zaragoza.[16] Similarly, Aragon had its own separate Holy Brotherhood, introduced into Ferdinand's realms in 1488,[17] where it operated until suspended by the Cortes of Tarazona in 1495.[18] In Catalonia there was yet another citizen militia group—the *Sometent*—that retained its individual character throughout our period.[19] It is also notable that neither Basque, Aragonese, nor Catalan militias fought alongside the Holy Brotherhood of Castile in Granada despite the supposed unity of the Christian effort.

In summation, the crown had total command of the Castilian Council of the Holy Brotherhood. The control it exercised over the hermandades through this Council was a good deal less absolute. The crown could not carry decisions without municipal cooperation, nor could it appoint or remove lesser officials. In the age of Ferdinand and Isabella, the curse of Iberian separatism, both within Castile itself and between Castile and the other kingdoms, was not overcome, even for the hermandades.

6

The Militia:
Taxation and Structure

Taxation

ALONG with all other major officers of the Council of the Holy Brotherhood, financial officials held co-relative posts in Isabella's royal government. As a result the general fiscal policies of the realm were adopted for use in the brotherhood structure. Ferdinand and Isabella made a number of changes in the royal fiscal and collecting functions during their reign. The informal financial council they inherited, composed of the chief bookkeepers and officers of the treasury and the royal domain, was early divided into one office for the treasury itself and one for royal accounts, presided over by their respective bookkeepers.

One of these royal bookkeepers, Alfonso de Quintanilla, was given charge in 1476 of directing taxation for the Council of the brotherhood.[1] Quintanilla and his assistant Juan de Ortega, the general administrators, together with their small staff of lawyers and accountants, supervised the tax farmers whose job it was to gather taxes and fines levied by brotherhood alcaldes from municipal and provincial treasuries.[2] The work of these general administrators grew constantly as the brotherhood moved from being a temporary expedient to becoming a permanent adjunct to the government. In the early years (1476–1478) administrative policies were relaxed. There were no definite assessments and no deadlines set.[3] But in 1478 Ferdinand obtained the first long-term (three years) fiscal commitment from the municipalities.[4] Henceforth specific assessments were set from August 15 (Santa Maria de Agosto, the feast of the Assumption, was the usual date for rendering grain payments) to August 15 and were made payable thrice yearly. The due dates were September 1, January 1, and May 1.[5] To assure that the quotas be met on time, the administrators engaged in heavy correspondence with

NATIONAL BUDGETS

Year (August to August)	Ordinary (in maravidís)	Extraordinary (in maravidís)	Total (in maravidís)
1478–79	17,800,000[a]	——	17,800,000[a]
1479–80	17,800,000[a]	——	17,800,000[a]
1480–81	17,800,000[a]	——	17,800,000[a]
1481–82	17,800,000[a]	[g]	
1482–83	17,800,000[a]	[h]	
1483–84	17,800,000[a]	10,000,000[i]	28,000,000
1484–85	17,800,000[a]	12,000,000[j]	29,800,000
1485–86	32,000,000[b]	12,000,000[k]	44,000,000
1486–87	32,000,000[c]		
1487–88		[l]	
1488–89	33,675,000[d]	——	
1489–90		——	
1490–91	33,870,000[e]	24,125,000[m]	58,000,000[m]
1491–92	33,525,000[e]	24,125,000[m]	64,000,000[m]
1492–93	33,450,000[e]	——	33,450,000
1493–94		——	
1494–95		——	
1495–96		——	
1496–97	34,500,000[f]	——	
1497–98	34,500,000[f]	——	34,500,000[f]

a. Estimate based upon percentage rise from household assessments of 1476 to assessment of 1485 cited in note b.
b. Clemencín, *Elogio de la reina,* p. 138. Original source not cited.
c. Aguado Bleye, *Manual de historia* vol. 2, p. 202. Original source not cited.
d. AGS *Contaduría de sueldo,* 1ª ser., leg. 53.
e. AGS *Contaduría del Sueldo,* 1ª ser., leg. 128.
f. Estimate based upon a letter from Quintanilla to the concejo of Seville, dated July 8, 1497, showing a rise in the provincial assessment due to seventeen newly incorporated concejos. AMS *Tumbo,* book 5, fols. 81–83.
g. Monetary figures not available. Navy raised by Andalusia and Galicia (1481–1482). AGS *Contaduría del Sueldo,* 1ª ser., fol. 10.
h. Monetary figures not available. Provincial Assemblies of Burgos and Madrid provided 16,000 beasts and 8,000 drovers. Azcona, *Isabel,* p. 508. Original source not cited.
i. Vote of General Assembly of Miranda del Ebro, November 1483 from ordinary fund. Serrano, *Burgos,* p. 185. Original source: AMB, 1483, fol. 55.
j. Vote of General Assembly of Orgaz, November 1484. Serrano, *Burgos,* p. 186. Original source: AMB, 1485, fol. 3.
k. Vote of General Assembly of Torrelunga, December 1485. Serrano, *Burgos,* p. 186. Original source: AMB, 1485, fol. 4.
l. Monetary figures not available. General Assembly of Fuentesaúco, March 1487. Levy of 10,000 peons with pay for eighty days. Azcona, *Isabel,* p. 516. Original source not cited.
m. Total for 1491 and 1492 includes a contribution from Galicia in 1491. AGS *Contaduría mayor,* 1ª época, leg. 134.

laggard taxpayers.[6] We find few admonishments directed at individuals, the bulk of the letters being addressed to concejos and communities.[7] The term community does not refer only to the Catholic Christian majority. The Jewish[8] and Moorish[9] population collected separate assessments to pay their communities' share of the province's quota.

By dint of these efforts, large sums were obtained. From the beginning Ferdinand and Isabella set their sights high. A memorial circulated in 1476 to the representatives at the first General Assembly estimated that more than sixty million maravedís a year could ultimately be collected from all the cities in the realm.[10] As may be seen from the table of national budgets, this prediction was fulfilled in the last years of the Granada War.

Monetary value in this table is presented in maravedís (mrs.). Originally a small silver coin, the maravedí had so declined in value that it disappeared from use and was retained only as a unit of account. At the start of Ferdinand and Isabella's reign there was great confusion in the coinage and continuous inflation. The gold *enrique*, standardized in 1471 at 420 maravedís and devaluated in 1473 to 400 maravedís, was not replaced until 1497. Then in the first coinage standardization of the reign, the enrique was displaced by a new gold *excelente de Granada* (or *ducate*, as it was modeled after the Venetian ducat) set at 375 maravedís.

Although prices and wages expressed in modern value are misleading, 1,000 maravedís of the late fifteenth century were equal to $6.95 in pre-1934 gold dollars. A million maravedís (some 3,000 ducates) were thus worth less than $7,000. Although a maravedí was not worth a cent in specie value, it had great purchasing value. A bushel of wheat (1493) cost seventy-three maravedís. A laborer could earn about 7,500 maravedís (20 ducates) a year. Sums raised by the brotherhood were thus not inconsiderable.[11]

With regard to assessments, the basic tax quota for support of the brotherhood structure was called the "ordinary" contribution (although it was actually extraordinary, being over and above the regular taxation paid for the maintenance of the brotherhood police). When a third level of taxation was added on for the Granada War, the word "extraordinary" was finally applied.

Under the Council's guidance successive General Assemblies determined the quotas of each province. The basic tax for maintenance of the militia was a levy on households, as opposed to one on individuals. In 1476 it was set at 10,000 maravedís per 100 households,[12] increased in 1485 to 18,000,[13] and remained unchanged until the abolition of the Council.[14]

To meet their quotas the provinces had to supplement this basic levy with excise taxes on merchandise and foodstuffs. A fairly complete runoff of figures can be assembled for Seville as a guide to the other provinces, bearing in mind that a national budget for 1491 to 1493 shows Seville to have paid about twice the quota of any other province.[15] The yearly "ordinary" quota for the city of Seville and its lands was set at 1,600,000 maravedís.[16] The ordinary assessment of the province of Seville (which includes the city and its territories) is listed in the table of assessments for Seville.

Assessments for the province of Seville

August to August	maravedís
1478 - 1481	4,375,970 [17]
1487 - 1490	4,341,810 [18]
1490 - 1493	4,887,540 [19]
1493 - 1496	4,971,690 [20]
1496 - 1499	5,368,790 [21]

Despite smooth functioning of the basic quota system in Seville, the general administrators did not develop a consistent tax policy. When the monarchs wanted extra funds they might go to a General Assembly and request a special subsidy, or they might entirely bypass the assembly, as they did in 1483, and appeal directly to the provincial assemblies of Burgos and Madrid.[22] They might even tap a city directly as in 1488 when the municipal council of Seville was requested to provide 5,000 foot soldiers and 500 cavalrymen from among its citizens, grandees, and brotherhood.[23]

The Council gave provincial officials much leeway to decide how these quotas would be met, what taxes would be levied, and who would contribute. The city of Seville again offers a well-documented example. In June 1478, the city fathers complained to Quintanilla and Ortega that hidalgos and clerics were not paying their share of the city's assessment.[24] Since the monarchs had reconsidered the wisdom of trying to tax the exempt estates, the Council could only recommend to the city that the deficit be made up by excise taxes on wines and fresh and salted fish.[25] The city then sought other revenue by proposing to obtain 150,000 maravedís a year from custom house brokers.[26] When the Council approved this plan a storm of protest erupted from the town's ninety-seven brokers. At a meeting on July 5 with the treasurer of Seville, the brokers had their way, obtaining several concessions that must have halved the projected contributions.[27]

Failure to cope with the gentry, the clergy, and the brokers aggravated the natural tendency of the city fathers to tax the least politically significant sectors of the population. When the city could not meet its quota again in July of 1479 it placed a surtax on every pound of meat sold.[28] Other taxes were levied upon every kind of petty craftsman and peddler.[29]

When quotas rose in 1485, harsh pressure was placed upon the urban economies. The city of Seville complained in 1487 that its commerce was being badly damaged by the taxes it had been forced to levy upon goods.[30] All the council could suggest was that the corporation try more food taxes (on bread, wine, meat, fruit, and fish), which might prove less controversial.

The temptation became irresistible to look outside the community for taxable sources. Traveling merchants offered a tempting prospect for revenue, although there was a royal ban upon the brotherhood's levying duty on merchandise entering or leaving cities.[31] Despite this prohibition the practice became widespread. Southern cities, like Seville and Cordova, which bore the heaviest responsibilities in the war, in desperation taxed visiting traders from northern commercial centers like Valladolid and Burgos.[32]

The Council responded to the bitter complaints of these merchants in a piecemeal fashion. Letters were dispatched to offending cities in answer to these petitions, but as the war approached its climax in 1491, incidents mushroomed.[33] Even after the war the Council provided only haphazard protection to traveling merchants, and not until 1495 did the crown "discover" that Seville was still illegally taxing these traders. It became necessary to reenunciate the original ban.[34] We cannot adjudge this action as being very beneficial to merchants because most brotherhood taxes were eliminated within three years.

Despite the war's being concluded, the Council had been continuing to collect the full quotas. At last, in 1496, to mitigate the pain of taxation for a new royal militia, contributors to the new force were excused from some brotherhood taxation.[35] Two years later contributions to the national quota were eliminated when the Council disbanded.[36] The Council was dissolved in June but taxes lingered through August.[37] Even at the end of the year the books could not be closed. In Seville, the monarchs had to appoint an official to aid royal treasurer Alonso Gutierres to check on debts owed and also to pay remaining bills.[38] It would be instructive to know what happened to the money left in the brotherhood treasury. Was it absorbed by the royal treasury or divided up and returned to the local police?

Two decades of treasury activity saw many drains against funds collected. One was the salaries of officials, high and low. In 1498 the yearly salaries of alcaldes and archers of Seville alone amounted to 800,000 maravedís.[39] The militia everywhere was equally well paid. A man-at-arms received 24,000 maravedís, a light cavalryman 18,000, and a footsoldier 15,000 maravedís a year.[40] Ferdinand and Isabella made sure a common soldier might complain directly to the crown if he was being cheated.[41] The provincial captain received in salary 1,000 maravedís a year for each lance he commanded and sometimes added to this by illegally keeping his company under roll call size, and then absorbing the extra salaries.[42] High-ranking officials did somewhat better. Ortega, for example, received a salary of 300,000 maravedís in 1494.[43] A sidelight on these extravagances is a curious bill in 1490 from Pulgar, the chronicler, for a velvet coat due him each year.[44]

Another continuous tax outflow was the service payment for the Jewish tax farmers. It was inevitable that the Jewish community in Castile, which involved itself in all of the crown's financial affairs, would also figure in this area. The chief royal tax farmer, Abraham Seneor, was appointed treasurer-general of the brotherhood in 1488 to administer all receipts and expenditures.[45] The previous year Rabbi Meir Melamed had succeeded his aged father-in-law as the chief administrator of tax farming. Together they worked as general receivers (*arrendador e recaudador mayor*) for the Council.[46] In 1490 Luis de Santagel, an Aragonese Jew who was chief treasurer of Aragon, and Francisco Pinelo, magistrate of Seville, took over these functions.[47] Not until after the Granada War and the expulsion of the Jews did the monarchs fully change brotherhood tax collection from a private into a government function.[48]

The financial drain for the farmers was forty-five maravedís for every 1,000 collected (fifteen for themselves, fifteen for their assistants, and fifteen for the local councils). In Galicia and Asturias they themselves received five maravedís less.[49] The farmers were personally enriched, we might estimate, by over four million maravedís a year at the height of the war.

In addition to the percentage allotted to the farmers, funds were also channeled away from treasury coffers in a third way. Through an arrangement made with the provinces in 1485 at the General Assembly of Torrelaguna, Isabella agreed to return to the municipalities one-fortieth part of the ordinary contribution collected, as a premium for improving local justice.[50] This attempt to neutralize opposition to the high cost of the war may have cost the treasury a million maravedís per year. Finally, the monarchs made a costly mistake in 1480 when they acquiesced to requests from the cities that they be relieved of a tax called *pedido y moneda*. In a memorial in 1500, Pedro Fernández de Toledo demonstrated that by agreeing to the cities' request the crown lost twenty million maravedís a year.[51]

Despite mistakes and extravagances the tax system of the Council was productive—so much so that the monarchs began to use brotherhood alcaldes to help in collecting other levies. The brotherhood Council worked with the Council of the Bull of Crusade[52] and with the Mesta, the sheep owner's guild.[53] Most important of all, the brotherhood entirely freed Ferdinand and Isabella from the vexation of having to call a single Cortes between 1482 and 1489.[54] In return for minimal political concessions, the brotherhood never failed to give the monarchs what they wanted in funds and troops for the long assault upon Granada.

Military Structure

A frequent conclusion drawn from the royal proclamation of the 1476 Cortes of Madrigal was that Ferdinand and Isabella's primary interest in creating their brotherhood lay in improving justice. Other brotherhood ordinances of the same year, drawn up at Chigales and at the first General Assembly at Dueñas, have not often been consulted.[55] By these laws a militia for the brotherhood was brought into existence. The creation of this force, not for justice but to meet immediate military requirements of the War of Succession, was Ferdinand and Isabella's overwhelming preoccupation in 1476.

By midyear all communities were ordered not only to build up their rural police to one light horseman per 100 householders and one man-at-arms per 150 householders[56] but in addition they were to set aside some troops to be kept on call for a militia.[57] It is difficult to tell if the militia was freshly recruited or formed from forces already at hand and renamed. In Burgos, at least, the latter was the case. To meet its first quota in 1476, the city corporation divided up existing police, earmarking twenty cavalrymen and ten foot soldiers for royal duty.[58] In any case, during lulls in the War of Succession, only a blurry line of separation was maintained between forces reserved for police action and the segment allocated to militia captains.[59] In its communications with the new force, the crown itself appeared uninterested in a special role for the militia. We find Council letters going directly to militia captains in 1477 and 1478 calling for petty investigations or imprisonments, similar to directives issued to the alcades.[60]

We can, however, already see the outline of royal control over the militia. Ferdinand, as king, retained personal control over all military forces of the realm, but appointed captain-generals to the charge of regional or other important commands.[61] Royal control was thus implicit in the 1476 appointment of his brother, Alonso de Aragón, duke of Villahermosa, to the Council as captain-general, or supreme commander, of the brotherhood militia.[62] It is difficult to determine exactly the size of the militia that the duke was to govern.[63] A force of about 3,000 men would be an authoritative estimate.[64]

Cavalrymen were still the elite troops during the fifteenth century. Heavy cavalry, however, was scarce in Castile, as in the rest of Europe, because it was expensive and horses were not abundant. It cost 8,000 maravedís to fully equip a man-at-arms with heavy plate, mount him on an armored steed, and provide him with a lance or a crossbow.[65] Two-thirds of the militia cavalry were the lighter, cheaper *jinetes* who rode their surefooted Arabian steeds with feet lightly planted in short stirrups.[66] They were provided, at a cost to the community of 7,000 maravedís, with a visored helmet (*capacete* or *babera*) and a lance, plus light armor that protected the chest, abdomen, arms, and legs.[67] The infantry played as yet a subordinate role, providing tactical support for the mounted troops. Each footsoldier wore a light breastplate (*coraza*) and a helmet (*casquete*). He carried a shield, a dagger, and either a pike or a crossbow.[68] This little army played a minor but helpful role in aiding Isabella's consolidation of power.

There appears to have been only the most haphazard kind of organization in this early force. The mounted troops were divided among the supreme commander and his eight provincial captains in disparate contingents of 300, 200, and 100 lances.[69] In 1478 General Assembly approval was obtained for a three-year extension of the league. With secure financing, Ferdinand and his aides began to shape their forces into a more useful tool. At a troop muster held in 1480, fourteen companies appear to have been created (at least for payroll purposes). These fairly uniform companies consisted of a captain (*capitán principal*), one ensign (*alférez,*) two trumpeters, two drummers, and 100 lancers.[70] There is also an indication in the legislation of the General Assembly of Madrid of a standard division of these 100 lance companies into four parts, each led by a lieutenant (*hombre principal*).[71]

Key to royal control of subordinate aspects of this command pyramid lay with provincial captains. Initially they were elected and paid by the municipalities.[72] It was necessary for the Council to choose and pay these men itself before royal control could extend to the ranks.[73] The captains of 1480 represent the start of the triumph of central authority over localism, of continuity over anarchy. During the Granada War they become leaders in their own right and start to receive prominent notice alongside the lords.[74]

The crusade completed the separation of the militia from the local police and put it completely under royal control. Nothing was better suited for rallying the country behind the young monarchs in selfless surrender of parochial interests than a Holy War. An act of Muslim aggression in 1481 against the Christian garrison of Zahara, a small fortified town north of the Andalusian border, furnished the necessary pretext for war. In the first months of the war the monarchs concentrated upon gaining the cooperation of the hermandades in the problem of supply. The Christian struggle in the mountainous terrain of the south was hampered by transportation problems of enormous magnitude. The first campaign personally directed by Ferdinand was a revelation of the difficulties that lay ahead. He found in June 1482 that it had taken him four months to capture two tiny cities.

Food, supplies, cannon, all had to be hauled up craggy slopes as the war settled into long campaigns of seige and attrition. The brotherhood played an important role in obtaining the beasts of burden needed by the quartermaster corps. In December 1482 the General Assembly of Pinto requisitioned 16,000 mules, donkeys, and horses for a spring campaign.[75] Here was a clear indication to the brotherhood that its organization had moved into new spheres.

Another action the monarchs took was to call up the militia, which since the close of the civil war had been assisting local police in crime fighting. From 1482 the militia was drawn away from the provinces where they had been raised as the need arose. This irregular practice was formalized at the important General Assembly of Torrelaguna (1485) when the militia's duties were confined to the war.[76] Moves were also made to recruit more men for the infantry through the auspices of the brotherhood. These men were to serve as soldiers or laborers (diggers, drovers, carpenters, and pillagers). The infantry contingents year by year grew in size:

1483	Assembly of Pinto	8,000[77]
1485	Assembly of Torrelaguna	5,000[78]
1487	Assembly of Fuentesauco	10,000[79]
1488	Assembly of Arranda	10,000[80]
1489	Assembly of Tordesillas	10,000[81]
1490	Assembly of Adamuz	10,000[82]

To deal efficiently with so many men the infantry was organized into companies in 1488. Significantly, the decree to do so was issued by the monarchs and only thereafter approved by the General Assembly of Arranda.[83] Ten thousand foot soldiers were arranged into twelve equal companies, each in function and size like a regiment.[84] Each company had its captain and an administrative staff of an alcalde, a purser, and a treasurer. The fighting men numbered 800; 720 were pikemen and eighty carried muskets (*espingarderos*). This group was broken down into fifty-man squads (*cuadrilleros*) led by squad leaders.[85]

The infantry of 1488 was the culmination of a decade of innovation. The brotherhood militia was the only large-scale force available to Ferdinand as a military laboratory wherein new experiments could be tried with a minimum of opposition. One of the first improvements was in discipline. To rally the troops, he gave each company a standard bearer and eight drummers.[86] The drum, of Oriental origin, made its first appearance in Europe in the middle of the fifteenth century. Its hypnotic cadence aided the transition of the military from the colorful diversity of chivalry to the drab uniformity of modern arms. The brotherhood militia was in advance of its age in other ways. All the men were dressed uniformly. From 1485 the soldiers wore a crusader costume to carry out the theme of Holy War. The outfit consisted of red trousers, a loose white jacket with a blood red cross on the breast, a silver-colored pointed helmet, and a sword marked with another red cross.[87]

Moves were also made toward the standardization and improvement of arms. The standard pike, adopted from Swiss and German models, was almost fourteen feet long. These pike-carrying militiamen were not yet the fearsome infantry of Spain's Golden Age. In the broken terrain of Granada they formed an effective, fast-moving body. The tactics they developed, however, when tried in Italy by the great Captain Gonzalo Fernández de Córdoba, failed disasterously on the open plains in confrontation with heavy French cavalry and the longer pikes of the Swiss.

Missile-firing arms were in a period of even more rapid change. Throughout the period under discussion the brothers carried a simple crossbow with a straight, rectangular shaft. It was spanned either by hand or by the foot on a girdle strap. The quarrels (they are never called arrows) had a warhead with a diamond or leaf shape. They were carried in a short, wide quiver hung across the back. The crossbow was an armor-piercing weapon of great value because anyone could quickly learn to load and fire the weapon accurately. It was effective but on its way to obsolescence.

By the second quarter of the sixteenth century almost all European rulers would replace the crossbow with a powder musket. In 1488 a few militiamen carried an *espingarda* (a heavy, inaccurate firearm that was little more than a wooden stock, a long metal barrel with a touch hole, a pan for powder, and a burning rope to ignite the affair).[88] Men had to be trained to handle this new weapon, however, and the brotherhood infantry was an unskilled force of peasants. In order to get trained gunners the monarchs were pushed along the path of money commutation for military service. In 1480 they requested that the General Assembly send the equivalent of 700 salaries in place of men so that others could be hired who would be good marksmen.[89]

Having established the identity of the militia we might also see where it fit into the Christian army that captured Granada. Descriptions of this heterogeneous force read like passages from early medieval chronicles. The great bulk of troops arrived at battles under the personal leadership of the grandees or their lieutenants, as in times past. Supplementing them were levies from the Andalusian cities, soldiers of military orders, mercenaries, and foreign adventurers. After armies assembled, leaders allowed the monarchs to divide the forces into components of cavalry and infantry called "battles." In May 1489 Ferdinand held a review of his ten battles prior to an attack on the Muslim town of Baza.

> His host numbered 13,000 horse and 40,000 foot soldiers, whom he ordered drawn up as follows. He commanded that in the first line there should be 150 mounted men with the Alcalde of the Young Pages . . . in the vanguard should go the Grand Master of Santiago with 1,800 lancers, with whom went the men of Ecija with 150 lances and 700 foot soldiers and 150 *espingarderos* of the city of Toledo. At one wing of this battle he placed the Grand Master of Calatrava with 400 lances and 1,000 foot soldiers. And at the other wing marched Pedro López de Padilla with 200 lances. . . . In the fourth battle went the horse and foot soldiers of the Brotherhood, each squadron with its captain. . . . In the tenth battle went Don Alonso, lord of the House of Aguilar, with 300 lances and 300 footsoldiers. . . .[90]

The groups were constituted according to no rational system of size or type of arms but according to origins. Out of this welter of diverse troops, two distinct elements can faintly be discerned that might be called the "feudal" and the "royal" components. This latter group included the brotherhood, the orders, and the mercenaries. Understandably, Ferdinand preferred soldiers under his personal control who could be used in sensible formations under a unified command.[91]

The person of Ferdinand provided one element of unity for the royal contingent. Another unifying force for the royal contingent during the war came from the merger of the Council of the Holy Brotherhood with the council of the constable. The once powerful office of constable, which had been established in the fourteenth century to act for the king as a general military commander, was held by Pedro Fernández de Velasco. This working arrangement was facilitated when the brotherhood Council was moved from Toledo to Burgos, which was the seat of the constable.[92] Joint signatures are found on documents from 1487 that pertain to brotherhood business, with no discernible pattern of separate responsibilities.[93] The constable's name is found as often in letters concerning taxation and justice as in military affairs.[94] The inclusion of the constable on the Council of the Holy Brotherhood indicates that by the end of the Granada War the Council had become primarily a military planning committee. All attention was focused upon financing and directing the activities of the militia, which had blossomed out in a full-scale royal army with cavalry, infantry, and even artillery.[95]

After the great victory the prudent monarchs looked for ways to preserve and consolidate this army. Quintanilla was requested to study the infantry problem. The excellent brotherhood militia had had its defects. At its peak strength it was never a satisfactory standing army. The term standing army presumes certain conditions: a permanent body of professional soldiers, whose expenses are assumed in full by the nation and who will fight wherever needed. The brotherhood infantry does not fit this definition even if these guidelines are loosely applied. As to permanence, mass levies were requested by the monarchs only for particular campaigns, and General Assemblies authorized only eighty days' pay for the peasants.[96] Further, the state was not assuming the full financial burden as the monarchs were personally responsible for provisioning these men once raised.[97]

The militia served the queen well in conflicts close to home but was a less than perfect instrument for an aggressive foreign policy. Significant use of the brotherhood was never made beyond Castile's shores. A small troop detachment assisted in the conquest of the Canaries (1482)[98] and a few pike men sailed with Columbus on his second voyage.[99] Despite these exceptions, the brotherhood functioned primarily as a defensive force for the cities. Even its activities in Granada, which appear to go beyond tradition, were sanctioned by centuries of hermandad strife with the Moors. It is unlikely that the monarchs, powerful as they were, could have coerced the municipalities to send their forces to fight outside the homeland, for example, into Italy. Yet Ferdinand's interests there were slowly and inevitably forcing Spain into conflict with France. If Spain was to play a great role in Europe, a mobile army equal to that of France had to be created.

The plan that Quintanilla drew up called for the Council to undertake an accurate census of the Castilian population able to carry arms.[100] This was important because his experience demonstrated that frauds, tricks, and bribes had caused inaccurate apportionments. A million men between the ages of twenty and forty were presumed to be available. When called, the troops were to be paid by the towns until they arrived at assembly points. During their absence their municipalities would be responsible for the care of their families. The magistrate of each province was to take an inventory of men, artillery, and of the arms that each trained individual was supposed to maintain. The lists were to be sent to the Council where they would be compiled and presented to the monarch.[101]

These thoughtful proposals were put away until the first Italian war broke out in 1495. It then became imperative that the sort of army Quintanilla envisioned be created. The Catholic Sovereigns would have to give up the brotherhood militia, as cities presumably would not be willing to pay for both forces. On May 3, 1495, a call was issued for a General Assembly, instructing delegates to be prepared to end brotherhood taxation.[102] In June, before the assembly met, the king held a meeting of Castilian city officials at Santa Maria del Campo, during which plans for an army constructed along the lines of Quintanilla's proposal were approved.[103] All citizens were ordered to provide themselves with arms, complying with standards established by prior brotherhood quotas.[104] Later in the month the General Assembly met in the same town and agreed to undertake the drafting and training of the new infantry.[105]

Under the desperate promptings of Gonzalo de Córdoba,

whose forces were being cut to pieces in Italy, the Council proceeded by early 1496 to draft one of every twelve male Castilians between the ages of twenty and forty-five not a cleric or otherwise exempted. Men taken for this new force were not required to serve in the brotherhood, and former brotherhood soldiers were excused.[106] The total force contemplated was 83,333 foot soldiers and 2,000 light cavalrymen *(caballos de lina)*.[107]

This giant militia was never used. P. J. Stewart, Jr., has made a major contribution to the study of the Holy Brotherhood by discovering that the new force never fully went into effect.[108] The Italian wars were soon over. No great national emergency followed and the Spanish army continued to be a haphazard affair of volunteers, rather than a standing militia.[109] It would appear from Stewart's evidence that Ferdinand and Isabella made a serious blunder. In return for suppressing the brotherhood militia in 1497,[110] the crown won a prohibitively expensive royal militia it could never afford to use.[111] It is ironic that after years of careful building, balancing off one institution against another in order to achieve what few European monarchs could boast, the Spanish crown was left in the end without either a brotherhood militia or a national army.

7

The Rural Police

KING ALFONSO X, the Learned, set his city of Ciudad Real as a buffer against the Moors on the high bare plains of La Mancha, midway between Toledo to the north and Cordova to the south.[1] In the closing years of the fifteenth century the town was still completely surrounded by high protective walls crowned with 130 towers. As necessary as the walls for protection of the city was its venerable ancient royal brotherhood.[2] This hermandad, one of many that existed during the lifetime of Ferdinand and Isabella's Council of the Holy Brotherhood, permits a look at the work of local police through an account book kept from October 1491 to September 1492 by Ciudad Real's majordomo.[3] After reviewing the constabulary operations of Ciudad Real, their relations with the Council will be analyzed.

A few examples of payments made to constables for expenses, drawn from the book for the last quarter of 1491, illustrate the range of petty activities that kept a brotherhood busy: thefts of chickens and hens, of a hooded cape, and of a crossbow; the destruction of some trees and their fruit; and a reward of five *reales* of gold to an archer who killed a mountain bear.[4] Brothers took part as well in all political and religious functions of their cities, and other records show how deeply woven they were in the social life of their municipalities.

The great events of Spain's *annus mirabilis*, 1492, break through the recitation of mundane disbursements only briefly. In the first entry in the majordomo's book for January, the capture of Granada is recalled as the scribe records 850 maravedís contributed by the brothers toward a bullfight and municipal festivities arranged in celebration of the event.[5] The brothers' full participation in the religious life of their city can be seen from the fact that they maintained a chapel in the principal church, Santa Maria del Pardo.[6] Each year they marched, under their own banner, in the solemn processions of *Espírito Santo* and *Corpus*.[7] Funds for these festivals and for charity contributions to a local monastery were granted freely from the brotherhood's full chest.[8]

Another aspect of the involvement of the brotherhoods in the civic life of their municipalities was their pride in erecting imposing buildings. The brotherhood police station in Ciudad Real, for example, was built on Dorado Street in the finest part of town. The upkeep of this attractive house was a major yearly expense. In 1492 the main rooms had to be repaired and a new set of doors installed.[9]

Unfortunately, today, the Ciudad Real house of the Holy Brotherhood has been incorporated into a larger municipal jail. In the nearby city of Toledo, however, a fine specimen of a hermandad police station has been restored to fifteenth century conditions. It is worth a visit to Toledo to recapture the era of Ferdinand and Isabella. On an uphill path behind the great cathedral of Toledo is a two-story building now called the Museum of the Holy Brotherhood. Over the doorway, Isabella's coat of arms is carved; to the right and left are her emblems, a yoke and a fan of arrows. At the very top of the doorpost is the coat of arms of Castile, held in place by a bat, whose ugly, ratlike head, with a halo around it, has been cleaned and restored.

The heavy wooden entrance doors, when thrown open, are high enough for mounted men to enter the dark vestibule. In the entrance, a faded map of the province, once the focus of hurried consultations, is painted on the left wall. After dismounting, the men divested themselves of saddles and riding trappings in a

Hermandad jail of Toledo prior to its restoration

Hermandad jail restored as Museum of the Holy Brotherhood of Toledo

tiny room and reported in to the large ground floor offices of the tribunal.

A prisoner being brought in for investigation might be taken at once up the heavy stone staircase to the huge chamber on the first floor. In the bare, white rectangle of the judges' hall, decorated only by two archers painted on a wall, the omnipotent alcaldes sat in judgment. When the alcaldes finished, a subterranean cell awaited the prisoner. In the far back of the building are four dark, cramped rooms and a bleak chapel that face on to a cheerless patio of rough gray stone.

Today, Toledo's Museum of the Holy Brotherhood slumbers, its cells empty. But in 1492 the brothers of Ciudad Real were doing their best to keep their city's jail cells full. Between October 1491 and October 1492 the principal responsibility for assuring that justice be done in Ciudad Real was in the hands of alcaldes Juan Ruys Cavallero and Christobal de Treviño. These hermandad alcaldes combined in their persons the functions of tax collector, police chief, and judge.[10] Their many specific responsibilities included the punishment of major crimes against society such as: the theft or destruction of property; physical violence, including murder and rape; and the harboring of criminals. During Isabella's reign their jurisdiction grew to incorporate crimes against the government such as: rebellion; usurpation of tax-gathering; private imprisonments (without the order of competent judges, for longer than twenty-four hours); and attacks on brotherhood officials or their representatives during General Assemblies. In addition to the enumerated duties the brotherhood had some broadly drafted mandates that put vast power into an alcalde's hands. Judges were instructed to imprison any suspect, and after collecting evidence the brotherhood officials alone were to decide if the criminal fell under their jurisdiction. The brotherhood was given the responsibility of recapturing and punishing all prisoners who escaped from jail after sentencing.[11]

In 1491–1492, in addition to Ciudad Real's two alcaldes, there was an executive council that consisted of six delegates. Elections were held every October for these posts, but continuity was as-

sured. The elders switched positions: a delegate one year had been
an alcalde the preceding term.[12] Direction of the executive council was assumed by one of the delegates, Mateo de Antequera, who
held the post of majordomo. Of the other delegates, at least one,
Juan de Villareal, is identified as a city alderman. Police ranks
were stable. The head constable, Juan Rodrigues de Marcos,
maintained a force of six lieutenants (Bartolomé de Bilboa, Alvaro
Bravo, Bartolomé Sánchez Cavallero, Louis de Molina, Cristoval
de Retamal, and Diego de Villalobos). *Peons,* persons without
rank, assisted the constables on their rounds.

There were several crimes that required many entries in the
majordomo's book, including a four-month investigation that
began in December of 1491 when a thief broke into the house of
Father Pablo Ferrandes, chaplain of the church of Santa Maria
del Pardo.[13] After the discovery of the robbery, the indignant
priest himself may have hurried to the police station, a few min-
utes walk from his church, and demanded that the brotherhood
take prompt action to recover his money and jewels. Thereupon,
the alcalde sent his runner to have another church sound alarm
bells to round up the constables, in much the same way that volun-
teer firemen are summoned today.[14] As soon as the police assembled at the jailhouse, they were informed of the details of the
theft of Father Ferrande's jewels, and then, mounted on fast
horses, they sped out of town in hot pursuit of the criminal. They
wore loose cloaks of forest green (characteristic color of the brotherhoods) trimmed with silver. A peaked green cap, a small white
ruff at the neck, pantaloons to the calf met by long hose, and
pointed leather shoes completed the costume. Their lead men bore
their standard of green damask worked with an arrow of metallic
thread, hung with tassels and cords of silk. During Isabella's reign
her arms, a golden yoke and banded black arrows, were added to
the flag.[15]

The men went wherever the criminal may have fled. It was
frontier country. Great flocks of merino sheep roamed in search of
pasture. The wastes were dotted with lightly settled communities
where strangers were regarded with fierce mistrust. Anyone from

another town, even the neighboring one, was an *extranjero,* a for-
eigner. To travel from one urban center to another involved risk.
Voyagers and merchants traveled in armed groups to protect
themselves from highwaymen. The nobility were often no better
than brigands, contemptuous of the untitled, quick to take insult,
and always ready with the sword. The area might be compared
with early settlements in North America's western states. The consequences of frontier life were vigilante justice in America and
hermandad justice in Castile.[16]

There was a high degree of cooperation between the Castilian
cities in the maintenance of this rough justice. As a band of brothers came to a town, the bells would be sounded, summoning the
brotherhood of that place, and with a great hue and cry the
augmented force would sweep forward. The original party was
only to pursue the quarry for five leagues and then drop out to
leave the chase to fresher men.[17] Theoretically, such pursuit might
even go as far as the borders of Aragon or Portugal.

In practice Ciudad Real's patrols tended to be short. Constable
Christoval de Retamal and his two peons pursued the thief of
the cleric's jewels for only four days during December 1491.[18]
Although their mission met with no success the brotherhood did
not drop the investigation. Constables went out on their assigned
rounds bringing with them their small tin boxes that contained
parchment warrants for suspects in all unsolved crimes.[19] Perse-
verence led to success. By March 1492, two women were discovered sheltering the thief in Fuentlabrada. Constable Bartolomé
Sanchez Cavallero and an assistant set off at once. The thief was
captured, but despite assistance from an archer assigned by the
authorities of Molinillo, the women could not be found. [20]

In April the Ciudad Real hermandad was called upon to solve
another church robbery. This was on a grander scale. A house of
worship had been broken into and desecrated. Among the valu-
ables taken were vestments of an image of Santa Maria de Guadi-
ana, including her valuable collar.[21] Elaborate ornamentation of
sacred images has long been an important feature of Spanish
Catholicism. It is not surprising that thefts were occasionally in-

cited by displays of dazzlingly soulful Madonnas clad in heavy silk gowns and priceless pearl trains, troubled brows encircled by finely-wrought golden crowns. In so important a case alcalde Juan Ruys Cavallero went along with the patrol. The men who went with him were tough, used to living out in the countryside and sleeping on the ground. When they were on a search such as this the brothers would assemble evéry evening before retiring to pray and to pledge their allegiance to the monarchs. Three times they recited loudly:

Dios, Ayuda! Santa Maria, Val!
E San Juan de Latran
E San Cristóbal de Las Aguas Pasar
E San Pedro de Ultramar
A los Reyes, Nuestros Señores
y á todos los que tienen y sostiene
La Santa Hermandad
de Toledo é Talavera é Ciudad Real. *

The alcalde replied each time "Amen," to end the day.[22] When no trace of the thief of the Virgin's collar could be found, the patrol returned after only two days.[23] Constable Diego de Villalobos was then sent out alone to scour the countryside along the hot, dusty April roads. The province of Ciudad Real suffers from parching heat in the summer. Even with irrigation its poor land is capable of only sparce vegetation—cereals, saffron, olives, and hardy vines. The constable returned after ten days without a prisoner.[24] This was only the most notable of many unsolved crimes in 1492. Out of twenty-three reported crimes in the majordomo's book, fifteen entries for 1491–1492 end with the doleful refrain

---

*Heavenly Father, help us! Holy Mary, favor us!
Saint John of Latran, favor us!
Saint Christopher of Las Aguas Pasar, favor us!
Saint Peter of Ultramar, favor us!
To the Monarchs, our Lords,
and to all who support and sustain
The Holy Brotherhood
of Toledo, Talavera, and Ciudad Real.

that the criminal escaped after a chase, evidence against traditional views that the Holy Brotherhood was a very efficient machine. Ferdinand and Isabella gave the police sufficient incentive to make arrests. After 1485 the archers received 1,000 to 5,000 maravedís per capture.[25] The ease with which criminals could avoid discovery necessitated close cooperation between the brotherhoods if anything at all was to be accomplished. Officers of Ciudad Real conferred regularly with their counterparts at Almagro and Chillon in order to settle disputes[26] and apportion taxes[27] The brothers of Toledo and Talavera met with Ciudad Real in the last quarter of each year to coordinate policy.[28] Reciprocity was practiced in the exchange of prisoners. For example, in March 1492 Ciudad Real conducted negotiations with the alcaldes of Real de Granada who had captured a suspected murderer, the only homicide reported for the year.[29] During September, the alcaldes of Ciudad Real traveled to the nearby pueblo of Chillon on a different matter, to examine a suspect, one Juan Ramiro, imprisoned on a charge of stealing a knapsack, a silk hood, and other items of value.[30]

The only judge ever seen by most suspects was likely the first alcalde who tried them. Justice was swift in the fifteenth century. When a brotherhood alcalde received a complaint, he was instructed to make an immediate imprisonment, if possible, on the basis of whatever information was available. A maximum of nine days was allowed for completing the investigation and rendering the verdict. During this time charges were to be published abroad by the town crier every three days so that all might be informed.[31] Once proceedings had commenced, they could not be stopped, even by a clash of jurisdiction or an appeal to the highest level of government.[32] Appeal was made very difficult, but in exceptional cases a plea could be carried as far as the queen's Royal Council of Castile, which was a court of final jurisdiction. The brotherhood of Ciudad Real spent a busy half year with one such plea. Early in April 1492, a complaint was made by a resident of the hamlet of Arrova against a native of Piedrabuena, Rodrigo de

Vargas. After taking testimony in a Piedrabuena inn, a constable arrested Vargas. Vargas spent four months in jail, but near the end of July an official of the royal court called for the records by order of the queen. The prisoner claimed the "privilege of crown protection," and he obtained results. For a month functionaries scurried about taking new testimony, and messengers went back and forth from the court, which was at Toledo. Finally, a delegation including a city alderman made the long trip from Ciudad Real to Vallodolid (where the peripatetic court had moved) and resolved the case.[33]

Despite the possibility of such appeal, alcaldes of the brotherhoods did not fear to mete out sentences to offenders as harsh as the trials were brief. The accused would be dragged up from his cell and brought to the whitewashed tribunal room, where behind an ornate table sat the judge who pronounced sentence. For petty theft of under 500 maravedís the penalty was a number of lashes. For a theft worth 500 to 5,000 maravedís, a leg or other member was severed from the body.[34] What passed for justice in Renaissance Europe was fierce indeed, but the Holy Brotherhood was regarded as harsh, even for those times. A physician at the royal court wrote of the years of Isabella's reign that:

> . . . justice was so severe that it appeared to be cruelty, but it was necessary because all the kingdoms had not been pacified, nor had the dominions of tyrants and haughty men been abased. And because of this there was much veritable butchery of men with the cutting off of feet, hands, shoulders, and heads, without sparing or disguising the rigors of justice.[35]

A common penalty was death. Since brotherhoods were prohibited from holding their executions in towns, Ciudad Real's scaffold was out in the bleak wilderness of Paralvillo.[36] A condemned person was trundled out to the field before dawn and tied to an upright post, his waist and legs made fast by wooden clamps. Ancient regulations prescribed that this post not be permitted to take the form of a cross.[37] The archers inserted crude iron darts into their wooden crossbows. As the sun rose, the firing squad lined up in front of the post. A priest might also be there to administer the last sacrament, as requested by the pious queen. Death, she hoped, would come quickly, to bring peace more securely to the soul.[38] Being shot by a cross-bow, however, was a slow, barbarous way to die. Not often did the arrows straightaway find their mark. In significant crimes a prize was even awarded to the archer who first hit the heart. After death came, the broken bodies were abandoned in the open field to birds of prey.

The brotherhood was greatly hated because of the rigor of its penalties. Even the Inquisition was regarded as more merciful because an individual condemned by the Holy Office was strangled before the painful official punishment was administered. It wasn't until 1498 that the merciful queen extended this practice to the brotherhood.[39] The brotherhood, however, persisted in its old ways. In 1532 Charles V was petitioned that the regulation be observed:

> Since those who are condemned by the Brotherhood to be shot with arrows are shot alive, without first being strangled, as this seems to be inhuman, and sometimes causes a lingering death, we beg your Majesty to give orders that no one be shot with arrows without first being strangled, since this is the custom with heretics.[40]

In Ciudad Real in 1492 crimes that ended in executions were not an everyday matter. The year was taken up mostly with domestic squabbles and petty thefts of clothing and mules. Typical was the final complaint that majordomo Mateo de Antequera recorded before his term expired. This complaint concerned one Juan de Rodrigo, a peasant from Noves, who swore out a charge against his wife Maria and another peasant with whom she had absconded, taking her husband's donkey and mower. Typically, too, the missing couple could not be located.[41]

In reviewing the daily activities of a single brotherhood, one is struck by the fact that most business appeared to be handled at the lowest levels without constant supervision by the royal court. Despite the existence of the Council of the Holy Brother-

hood, it is possible that some ancient, privileged brotherhoods retained a degree of autonomy.[42] By this reasoning a case for the
retention of some independence might be made for Ciudad Real.
In 1418 John II approved the ordinances, good uses, ancient customs, privileges, liberties, and immunities of the brotherhood.[43] In
a brief decree issued on December 14, 1485, Isabella renewed her
father's letter of privilege without modification, and later charter
confirmations (1512, 1518, and 1528) seem to indicate the continued renewal of invested rights.[44]

The account book shows very limited contact between the city
of Ciudad Real and the crown: in October 1491 the alcaldes attended a General Assembly at the court "about the reformation
of the archers and the election of the officials of this brotherhood";[45] a minor royal official visited the majordomo in August
1492 regarding a complaint made at court;[46] and in September, a
city official saw the chancellor at court about the review of a
case.[47] Similar to all the brotherhoods examined, Ciudad Real
acknowledged monarchial obligations by paying a quota for the
maintenance of the national hermandad militia[48] and contributing small sums to crown representatives throughout the year.[49]

The hermandad of Ciudad Real appears on balance to have
been self-sufficient. It negotiated with other brotherhoods and
with other communities as equals without clearing petty matters through the court. In its day-to-day routine it appears to
have operated with a free hand except when an individual's
appeal was carried to the crown.

Broadening the field of inquiry from Ciudad Real to all of
the local brotherhoods, we find that the Council's inability to
place all of them under complete control was a major failing.
The Council was far too understaffed to be able to watch over all
details. The general administrators sent detailed instruction to
provincial and municipal officials only regarding tax assessments
and troop quotas. On other matters they issued broadly drafted
commands. A typical letter calling for a reversal of provincial
or municipal practice, or for a disciplinary action against the
police, consisted primarily of an admonishment that the laws

of the brotherhood be obeyed in the matter under discussion. An appropriate passage from a book of ordinances or a clause from a law might be included to give point to the directive. Details of how the command was to be put into effect were not often specified. For example, it was brought to the queen's attention that Seville was not punishing usurers, despite a ban on lending at usurious rates. Her letter to the city's brotherhood, although it runs to over one thousand words, does not mention by name one offender or remiss official. The competent authorities are simply reminded of their responsibilities and told to follow the laws and ordinances of the kingdom, none of which are specified.[50] One presumes from these letters that the brotherhood was allowed some flexibility in the specifics of daily operations.

The consequence of an undermanned bureaucracy and local autonomy was abuse of office. In the petitions that flowed into court, a thread recurs over the years of improprieties charged to brotherhood officials of various communities. The most common complaints were charges of unwarranted and illegal taxation.[51] The return of impressed goods to communities[52] and individuals[53] was also petitioned. Despite complaints, alcaldes grew rich from fines and confiscations. In 1480 the General Assembly passed a sumptuary decree censoring alcaldes and their wives for wearing overelaborate clothing of silk and crimson cloth and heavy gold jewelry, visible proof of newfound wealth.[54]

In addition to fiscal abuses the queen's subjects complained to her about other problems. Pleas were made by the citizens of the village of San Martin de Trevejo about an alcalde from Valverde who committed crimes against their community,[55] and by the residents of Cevico who suffered violence at the hands of two alcaldes from Dueñas.[56] The archers were also guilty of indiscretions. Successive General Assemblies passed stringent regulations to tighten discipline. Brothers were reminded that they were to take orders from the alcaldes, who would castigate them if they disobeyed.[57]

A dramatic denunciation of hermandad abuses of this type was made by the queen two years after her Council was abolished. In 1500 Isabella recognized the pleas of the well-to-do residents of Seville that the brotherhood had run riot by reestablishing the abolished office of juez ejecutor for the city, because

> the alcaldes, archers, and other officials of Seville . . . had many times caused grievances and injustice to persons who appeared before them under the statutes of the Brotherhood. These grievances and sentences could not be remedied as both poor persons, and those of quality, could not complain to the alcaldes, nor could the litigants secure justice in our courts.[58]

The poor and lowly left no similar record to tell us of their suffering at the hands of the queen's Holy Brotherhood. They eventually found their champion in Cervantes. The first part of his masterpiece, *Don Quijote de la Mancha*, although published in 1605, has a portrait of the brothers of Toledo, Talavera, and Ciudad Real that would not be unfamiliar to an earlier age. Fear, hatred, and contempt were emotions often aroused by the Holy Brotherhood.

Sancho Panza was understandably agitated after his master disturbed a party of travelers on the highway to Seville. " 'Twill not be strange if they advise the Holy Brotherhood, who will lock us up, and by my faith we shall sweat our tails before we get out." His fear grew when the knight, suffering under another delusion, freed four galley slaves. Panza tried patiently to explain to his visionary companion that the next time they might be caught in a foolhardy act and shot on the spot. "I want you to realize that the Holy Brotherhood have no use for chivalries and wouldn't give two coppers for all the knights-errant in the world, and even now I seem to hear their darts whizzing past mine ears." But Quijote trembles not at these warnings. He spits out his creator's contempt in the very faces of the enemy, that "filthy and base-born crew! . . . [a] band not of officers, but of thieves, brigands with the license of the Holy Brotherhood. . . ."[59]

8

Conclusion

QUEEN ISABELLA bestowed high praise upon the Holy Brotherhood in the 1498 decree ending the life of its governing Council. She reminded her subjects that before the league came into being, disorder had reigned in the kingdom. Everywhere in the countryside there had been constant robbery, injury, and murder. A solution had been found, thanks to God's grace. With the consent of her grandees, her advisors, and the municipal representatives to the Cortes, anarchy was overcome; peace, justice, and tranquility were brought to the land by the hermandad, and through its good offices the kingdom of Granada had been restored to the Holy Catholic faith. These tasks completed, it was in the queen's mercy to at last free her subjects from the taxes and vexations they had for so long borne with such good results.[1]

In this decree Isabella did not exaggerate the achievements of her police. Although investigation found the rural police to be inefficient, they made up for this in tenacity and brutality. Both serious and petty crimes were punished with a barbarity unusual even in a century known for its stake and chopping block. The alcaldes were quick to judge, heedless of appeal, and immediate in the execution of penalties. The tranquility they brought to Castile was similar to the Pax Romana as described in Tacitus: "Where they make a desert, they call it peace."

Into the coffers of this organization flowed Castile's gold, a goodly percentage of which found its way to the Council's treasury. So useful was the brotherhood tax system, despite disorders and extravagances, that not once during the lengthy Granada conflict did the queen convoke a Cortes for funds. The Council wisely used this money to organize and equip a superior militia that proved itself against the Moors. This militia developed into a substantial army, uniformly dressed, organized into rational companies, and placed under a neat hierarchy of officers dominated by one commander-in-chief. Although this force disintegrated after the war, lessons learned during its existence were long usefully applied to its descendants. As one final service, the Council recruited and trained the first of the brotherhood militia's successors, a kingdomwide royal infantry.

In such achievements Isabella could find much satisfaction. Nearly a quarter century had passed since plans were first made for the league and its Council, and perhaps she herself had come to believe all had happened as the decree maintained. It is forgotten that her Castilian Holy Brotherhood was created not to secure tranquility but to gain a throne. Far from being thought a lawful monarch putting her lands in proper order, Isabella was regarded by her foes as a usurper defrauding her niece Doña Juana of a rightful inheritance. It was primarily troops that interested Isabella from the moment of her self-coronation in 1474. So long as the Portuguese remained a threat, Isabella needed fighting men for war and not police for peace. Too much attention has been devoted to the brotherhood's founding petition at the Cortes of Madrigal in 1476, a document dealing primarily with proposed police operations. Little notice has been given to the laws and proclamations of the General Assemblies of 1476 and following years that created and expended a militia for Isabella's cause.

Explanation of the creation of the league has continued to rely primarily upon the Cortes documentation and a few royal chronicles. A favored theory, cut from cloth that Isabella wove, has been that all the municipalities of Castile agreed to the league's creation because they wished to see a strong monarch who could take in hand Castile's troublesome nobility. Yet far from demonstrating united support for Isabella, her league started out as no more than a temporary alliance of her friends in only the central and northern Castilian cities. We find it took two years of exertion to reduce the gap betwen the 1476 Cortes' pretention of establishing a kingdomwide general brotherhood and the reality. Only as Princess Juana's cause collapsed were formerly unfriendly or neutral cities forced into the league. Ironically, by 1478, at the very moment the last cities of the east and south entered the league, important allied towns like Burgos and Toledo were already refusing their taxes and clamoring to get out.

Such complaints lead to the conclusion that those who gathered at Madrigal had never intended that the league they were there to form should weaken their own independence. General brotherhoods had often been initiated by monarchs, and allowing Isabella to nominate her choices to high governing posts in the confederation was but an extension of this tradition. As most aspects of finance, law, police, and militia were kept in local hands, it was expected that the new brotherhood would be little different from its predecessors. One term was all that was authorized the league, and taxpayers were expressly ordered to resist any unlawful demands made thereafter, even if requested by the governing body or Ferdinand and Isabella.

Objections began to be voiced from the moment that the cutting edge of Isabella's authority was sharpened. The harmony of the April 1476 Cortes disappeared by the first General Assembly meeting in July when costs were presented. It was all Isabella's men could do to keep this meeting from breaking up without result. The argument that the king of Portugal remained a threat proved sufficient, however, to enlist pledges of armed forces. They were grudgingly produced, and in August some of the founding cities had to be threatened with fines by the General Assembly to force them to assume their obligations. Whatever squabbling existed in the first years was hardly to be compared to the storm that grew when rumors of peace circulated. The time for testing wills came in 1479.

A treaty with Portugal was signed that year and many cities discontinued paying taxes, despite the reluctant approval they had given in 1478 for a new three-year commitment. They anticipated that tradition would be followed and the league promptly disbanded, but this time things were to be different. The brotherhood governing body proved loyal not to the cities but to the crown. The Council applied heavy pressure through every subordinate royal hermandad official to make sure that taxes were paid. Opportunity once lost can not easily be regained. Automatic continuance of the confederation was soon assured by the providential start of the Granada War. Yet even during those years of abundant appeal to faith and loyalty, the brotherhood continued unpopular with those who had to pay its costs. When Isabella at last saw fit to abolish the league, she knew full well what satisfaction she brought to her subjects.

There is little evidence for supporting the traditional argument that the Council used the brotherhood to suppress the grandees to the advantage of burghers. Implicit in this theory is an unacceptable view of a changing social balance between a rising middle class and a descending nobility. This is not borne out by recent historical studies that emphasize the ever-increasing wealth and prestige of the nobility during the Renaissance era. Although Isabella's highborn supporters disliked any strengthening of royal power, they acceded to the formation of a brotherhood to meet the Portuguese threat against their candidate. Then, like the men of the cities, the nobility found a triumphant queen more difficult to control than anticipated. When they learned they could not force an end to the league, they accepted the situation and ceased complaining. Part of the reason for their silence was that the brotherhood affected their interests only slightly. It seems unlikely that the queen ever intended to employ her league to intimidate her supporters. When brotherhood troops were thrown into action in the War of Succession, some battles were indeed fought against grandees, but these grandees were men who supported her rival. After this brief period neither the militia nor the police were mandated to threaten the aristocracy. Of course it should be remembered that the militia's forces were insignificant compared to the immense armies that could be mustered by great houses.

The status of the burghers might have been indirectly improved by the grandee's loss of some privileges during the life of the brotherhood. Illegal imprisonment was prohibited and alcaldes were to be permitted to enter estates to search for criminals, but little else was changed. Grandees retained their personal exemptions from taxes as did all the gentry. Subject peasants on noble lands were taxed at a lower rate than free men. Little was lost of seignorial judicial rights, and other than having to allow a few police onto their estates, the miniature kingdoms of the grandees went on as before.

Another favored theory that should be revised attributes bureaucratic centralization and national consolidation to the Council, innovative qualities often associated with the achievements of fifteenth century "New Monarchs." In reality the Council was loosely organized; it did not fully control all aspects of the league; and it made little contribution to Spanish unity. Its history is replete with temporary expedients, unresolved organizational tangles, and shifting responsibilities. Because the Council was staffed with prominent men, their high rank has led to an unwarranted assumption that the body was carefully structured. Yet the brotherhood Council was little more than an informal committee of the Royal Council of Castile, Isabella's principal governing agency for her realms. Many years passed before this committee was designated as the "Council of the Holy Brotherhood," but even then no pattern of exclusive responsibility ever emerged for its officers, who handled problems as they arose. Indeed, most routine business was conducted by only two members, Quintanilla and Ortega, the chief administrators, for whom brotherhood affairs were but a minor part of their responsibilities.

During the decades in which the Council guided the Holy Brotherhood, ad hoc innovation rather than long-term planning appears to have been the rule. Prior to 1476, ordinance books of previous leagues were circulated among important personages for approval, and then these laws were copied intact into the Cortes petition without any revolutionary innovations. The militia was to be only a portion of each municipality's regular hermandad constabulary pledged to Isabella's use when needed. These fighting men and their captains answered to local authority, remained in the provinces where they were raised, and were hardly to be distinguished from ordinary police. After 1478, when the league was renewed and taxes were regularized, some improvements in organization were undertaken. The captains, who had been selected and paid by their provinces, were converted into salaried crown employees. Separation of their forces from police duties was begun, although not completed until during the Granada War.

Only during the latter years of the crusade did the militia approach modern norms of central control and rational organization. Even then, it never developed into a satisfactory army of full-time professional soldiers entirely at the call of their royal masters. Assemblies only authorized mass levies for particular campaigns, paid the infantrymen for only eighty days in a year, and left provisioning up to the crown. Furthermore, significant use could never be made of this force outside Castile. The hermandades were too closely linked to internal pacification and border control for Ferdinand and Isabella to consider sending them to fight against the French in Italy. Instead in 1495 the monarchs acted upon a proposal Quintanilla had made earlier for replacing the militia with a mobile royal infantry raised by universal draft. Under Council direction the hermandades quickly undertook the selection and training of this new force, completing this task by 1496. In the following year the brotherhood militia was suppressed. This turned out to be an unfortunate error as its substitute was discovered to be so expensive to maintain that it was disbanded before ever being used.

The domination eventually gained by the Council over the brotherhood militia was not matched by a like degree of direction for the police. Quintanilla and Ortega never came to exercise a total control over the network of alcaldes and constables. Some of the more ancient prestigious brotherhoods retained a vital degree of independence, and it was always a struggle to keep in formation the loose confederation that bore the title of Santa Hermandad. These anarchistic groups often did not restrain their members from straying beyond jurisdictional limits set by law and from meddling in all aspects of ordinary justice. Corrupt and venal minor brotherhood officials, nominated and elected by their own kind, could not effectively be kept by the general administrators from outstepping their powers.

The hermandades gained such license because Isabella used them as weapons in the fight for her throne and as a means to pacify her new domains. The queen's sycophants made much of her love for justice, yet power was on occasion allowed to take precedence over rectitude. The hermandades were told they could reach into their cities (despite municipal statutes to the contrary) to punish dissenters to Isabella's dubious rule and to institute a campaign of terror against any who fell afoul of their broadly drawn jurisdictions. Although Isabella might look away while such injustices were perpetrated, her cities were not as indifferent. Bitter complaints against arbitrary justice or greedy alcaldes were ignored for the most part, although a patchwork of instructions and laws grew up to mitigate some abuses. Yet for a decade the crown accepted no solution that would control the police by reducing their omnipotent powers. The Granada War was well underway before the queen became persuaded that the goodwill of her subjects, which she needed to expand the militia, would best be obtained by restraining the police. At the 1485 General Assembly of Torrelaguna, the legal authority and immunities enjoyed by the hermandades were reduced to nearly the level existing before the league was organized. Diminishing the power of the alcaldes and their armed bands reduced their mischief-making potential but deprived the crown of the unique system that had provided Castile with a powerful weapon for enforcing uniformity.

Finance is another area where a less than perfect control of subordinate elements is revealed. In general, there simply was an insufficient number of trained officials in Isabella's government to direct effectively all aspects of setting, collecting, and verifying taxation. For example, although supervision of tax gathering was placed in Council hands, no better method of collection was devised than continued reliance upon extragovernmental tax farmers who came from the Jewish community. No planning was made for the government to assume this function until the eve of the expulsion of the Jews.

Beyond techniques of collection, all tax quotas had to be approved by General Assemblies. It was always possible for an assembly to deny funds or give less than requested, although Isabella's prestige usually silenced opposition. Still, large grants requested of assemblies during the Granada War gave the municipalities a lever with which to wrest concessions, such as the 1485 reformation of the league. Although assemblies determined general quotas for the provinces, the form in which these assessments might be levied was left to local option. In the face of united pressure from the high estates, Isabella had scrapped a plan for universal taxation; consequently most expenses devolved upon the shoulders of the municipal fathers who were left to their own inventiveness to meet imposts. Not unnaturally this meant the shearing of the least politically important sectors of their communities, while the powerful or the vocal were not disturbed. As quotas mounted during the Granada War, the municipal governments felt hard-pressed and began to tax previously "exempted" persons. The Council spent much time answering complaints from clergy and nobility about these misbegotten levies.

In evaluating the effectiveness of royal control over the Santa Hermandad, it does not appear that Ferdinand and Isabella's actions reveal an appreciation of the modern desiderata of a nation state. The Council can not bear the weight of theories which state that it was meant to unite Spain or even to make a lasting contribution to governmental centralization in Castile. Each of

Ferdinand and Isabella's different realms had some variety of municipal organization. There was a Basque league, an Aragonese brotherhood, and a Catalan force. Not only were these conferedations never merged, but despite the supposed unity of the faith, none of the troops belonging to these city-leagues fought alongside Castile's brotherhood militia against the Moors. Even within Castile there were no long-term unifying gains from its league. The useful police network returned to local control and the militia, so effectively built up, was abandoned to let the monarchs chase after a delusory great royal army. Stripped of responsibilities by 1498, there seemed no need to retain a useless Council, however well versed its members were in brotherhood procedures. The hermandades slipped clear, free again to do as they would.

Ferdinand and Isabella had no regret at the death of the Council because it had been for them but a helpful experiment in government that had outlived its time. However little the Council left behind, it may still be valid to consider it as a unifying factor, a spiritual force. The first duty of a Renaissance Prince was to keep the peace. Isabella's Council provided a royal peace, and by so doing restored an ancient direct contact between subjects and their ruler. When the brotherhood struck, it did so in the name of the queen, and on the brotherhood flag was her device, the yoke and the arrows.

Notes

Abbreviations

AGS	Archivo General de Simancas
AGS Contaduría Mayor	Contaduría Mayor de Cuentas
AGS Diversos	Diversos de Castilla
AGS Sello	Registro General del Sello de la Corte
AHN	Archivo Histórico Nacional, Madrid
AMB	Archivo Municipal de Burgos
AMS	Archivo Municipal de Sevilla
AMS Actas Capitulares	Cuadernos de Actas Capitulares
BN	Biblioteca Nacional, Madrid
fol.	folio
leg.	legajo (bundle)
ser.	serie (series)
v	vuelta (unnumbered back of numbered page)
1ª	first

Notes to the Introduction

1. Tarsicio de Azcona, *Isabel la Católica: Estudio crítico de su vida y su reinado,* Biblioteca de Autores Cristianos, No. 237 (Madrid: 1964), ch. 5.
2. J. H. Elliot, *Imperial Spain 1469–1716* (New York, 1964), p. 75.

Notes to Chapter 1

1. Evariste Lévi-Provencal, *Histoire de l'Espagne Musulmane,* 3 vols. (Paris, 1953), 3:153–162.

2. Professor A. H. De Oliveira Marques of the University of Florida (Gainesville), personal conversation in 1967.
3. Louis de Montalvo y Jardín, *Discurso sobre las hermandades de Castilla* ... (Madrid, 1862), pp. 10 f.
4. Julio Puyol y Alonso, *Las hermandades de Castilla y León* (Madrid, 1913), pp. 11 f; Antonio Paz y Mélia, "La Santa Real Hermandad Vieja y la Nueva Hermandad General del Reino," *Revista de Archivos, Bibliotecas y Museos,* vol. 1 (1897), p. 98.
5. Luis Suárez Fernández, "Evolución histórica de las hermanades castellanas," *Cuadernos de historia de España,* (Buenos Aires, 1951), 16:7 f.
6. Ibid., pp. 6 f.
7. Suárez Fernández, "Evolución histórica hermandades," p. 11. Original source: letter of brotherhood between Plasencia and Escalona in *Anuario de Historia del Derecho Español,* vol. 3 (1926), pp. 503–508.
8. Ibid., p. 8; Paz y Mélia, "Santa Real," p. 98; Manuel Colmeiro, ed., *Cortes de los antiguos reinos de León y de Castilla publicados por la Academia de la Historia,* 5 vols. (Madrid, 1863–1903), 1:169 f.
9. Suárez Fernández, "Evolución histórica hermandades," pp. 14–19.
10. Colmeiro, *Cortes de los antiguos reinos,* 1:186 f.
11. Suárez Fernández, "Evolución histórica hermandades," p. 20.
12. Colmeiro, *Cortes de los antiguos reinos,* 1:282–237.
13. Suárez Fernández, "Evolución histórica hermandades," p. 29.
14. Possibly formed by Ferdinand III, but the first sure date is 1300. Ibid., pp. 31 f. Original source: letter of the hermandad de colmeneros y ballesteros dated October 15, 1300 in the Biblioteca Nacional, Madrid, MS 13030, fols. 115v–117v.
15. Suárez Fernández, "Evolución histórica hermandades," pp. 33–38.
16. Cortes of Valladolid, October 30, 1351. Colmeiro, *Cortes de los antiquos reinos,* 2:2–6.
17. Cortes of Medina de Campo, 1370. Ibid., 2:186 f.
18. Suárez Fernández, "Evolución histórica hermandades," p. 41.
19. Cortes of Segovia, 1386. Colmeiro, *Cortes de los antiquos reinos,* 2:336–350.
20. Suárez Fernández, "Evolución histórica hermandades," pp. 41 f.
21. Cortes of Guadalajara, 1390; Cortes of Madrid, 1393; Cortes of Valladolid, 1451. Colmeiro, *Cortes de los antiguos reinos,* 2:425 f, 528; 3:609.
22. For example, Pedro Aguado Bleye, *Manual de historia de España,* 3 vols. (Madrid, 1954–1956; revised 1959), 2:201.
23. Lorenzo Galíndez de Carvajal, *Crónica de Enrique IV,* ed., and a study by Juan Torres Fontes (Murcia, 1946), ch. 65.
24. Puyol y Alonso, *Las hermandades,* pp. 71 ff.
25. Konrad Haebler, "Die Kastilschen Hermandades zur Zeit Heinrichs IV (1454–1474)," *Historische Zeitschrift* (Munich, 1904), 56:40 ff.

26. Ordinances of Castronuño, Puyol y Alonso, *Las hermandades,* pp. 107–125.
27. Ibid. 28. Ibid.
29. Diego Enríquez del Castillo, *Crónica de Rey Don Enrique el Cuarto,* ed., Cayetano Rosell y Lopez. Biblioteca de autores españoles, no. 70. (Madrid, 1878), ch. 87.
30. Ibid.
31. Azcona, *Isabel,* pp. 119 f. Original source: Archivo Histórico Nacional, Fondo Osuna, leg. 1860, fol. 26.
32. The pact of Toros de Guisando, August 1468.
33. Colmeiro, *Cortes de los antiquos reinos,* 3:794 f.
34. Diego Enríquez del Castillo, *Crónica de Rey Don Enrique el Cuarto,* ch. 86.
35. Orestes Ferrara, *Un pleito sucesorio: Enrique IV, Isabel de Castilla y La Beltraneja* (Madrid, 1945), p. 309.
36. Paz y Mélia, "Santa Real," p. 106; Haebler, "Die Kastilischen Hermandades," pp. 42 ff.
37. General letter of brotherhood, from Villacastin, dated July 8, 1473. Text published in Suárez Fernández, "Evolución histórica hermandades," pp. 72–78.
38. Ibid.

Notes to Chapter 2

1. Although the bulk of recent Spanish research about the Reyes Católicos still awaits translation, the following works in English provide introductions to the major new ideas: J. H. Elliot, *Imperial Spain 1469–1716* (New York, 1964); B. J. Keen, introduction to J. H. Mariéjol, *The Spain of Ferdinand and Isabella* (New Brunswick, N.J., 1961); John Lynch, *Spain Under the Habsburgs: Empire and Absolutism 1515–1598* (Oxford, 1964).
2. J. B. Stiges, *Enrique IV y la Excelente Señora: llamada vulgarmente Doña Juana La Beltraneja* (Madrid, 1913).
3. Gregorio Marañón, *Ensayo biológico sobre Enrique IV de Castilla y su tiempo* (Madrid, 1934).
4. Orestes Ferrara, *Un pleito sucesorio.*
5. Jaime Vicens Vives, *Historia crítica de la vida y reinado de Fernando II de Aragón* (Zaragoza, 1962). See pp. 283–287 for comparisons of original and rewritten documents used by Isabella's followers to convey the impression that she was the only legitimate queen of Castile from the moment of her self-coronation in Segovia.
6. Ibid., p. 389; Azcona, *Isabel,* p. 45; Elliot, *Imperial Spain,* p. 11.
7. Juan Beneyto Pérez, *Historia de la administración española y hispanoamericana* (Madrid, 1958), p. 277.
8. Julius Klein, *The Mesta: A Study in Spanish Economic History* (Cambridge, 1920), pp. 355 f.

9. Eloy Benito Ruano, *Toledo en el siglo XV: Vida política* (Madrid, 1961).

10. L. P. Serrano, *Los Reyes Católicos y la ciudad de Burgos: desde 1451 a 1492* (Madrid, 1943).

11. Mariéjol, *Spain of Ferdinand and Isabella,* pp. 25 f.

12. Benito Ruano, *Toledo,* pp. 122 f.   13. Ibid.

14. In Juana's camp in 1475 were the cities of Madrid, Zamora, Toro, and Castronuño. She could also rely upon the cities in the territories of her allies, the archbishop of Toledo, the marques of Arevalo, and the grand master of Calatrava. For a more exhaustive list see J. F. D. Valencia, *La guerra civil a la muerte de Enrique IV: Zamora, Toro, Castronuño* (Zamora, 1929).

15. Alonso de Palencia, *Crónica de Enrique IV.* Castilian trans. by Antonio Paz y Mélia, 4 vols. (Madrid, 1904–1908), vol. 4, bk. 24, ch. 6.

16. Ibid.; Julio Puyol, ed., *Crónica incompleta de los Reyes Católicos 1469–1476: según un manuscrito anómino de su época* (Madrid, 1934), p. 306 note.

17. Fernando del Pulgar, *Crónica de los Reyes Católicos,* ed., with a study by Juan de Mata Carriazo (Madrid, 1943), vol. 1, ch. 70.

18. The Brotherhood of Valdeolea, Campo de Suso, Campo de Yuso, Valderredible, Val de Bezance, and the five villages. Archivo General de Simancas, Registro General del Sello de la Corte, March 1475, fol. 220; The Ancient Royal Brotherhood of Toledo, Talavera, and Ciudad Real. April 1475, fol. 380.

19. Jorge Vigón Suero-Díaz, *El ejército de los Reyes Católicos: Hay un estilo militar de vida,* Colleccion de libros de actualidad politica, no. 13 (Madrid, 1953), p. 64.

20. Vicens Vives, *Historia crítica de Fernando II,* pp. 429 ff.

21. Ibid., p. 437.

22. Lorenzo Galíndez de Carvajal, *Anales breves del reinando de los Reyes Católicos,* Biblioteca de autores españoles, no. 70 (Madrid, 1878), p. 451.

23. Colmeiro, *Cortes de los antiguos reinos,* 4:2.

24. Mariéjol, *Spain of Ferdinand and Isabella,* pp. 137 f.

25. At the municipal session of the Burgos city council of March 30, 1476, a communication was read from the sovereigns announcing the establishment of the brotherhood for the kingdom. Serrano, *Burgos,* p. 172. Original source: Archivo Municipal de Burgos, 1476, fol. 10.

26. Colmeiro, *Cortes de los antiguos reinos,* 4:3–11.

27. Celestino López Martínez, *La Santa Hermandad de los Reyes Católicos* (Seville, 1921), p. 8. Original source not cited.

28. Colmeiro, *Cortes de los antiguos reinos,* 4:3–11.

29. AGS Diversos, leg. 8, fol. 1. First half also in Colmeiro, *Cortes de los antiguos reinos,* 4:3–11.

30. Colmeiro, *Cortes de los antiguos reinos,* 4:3–11.

31. Galíndez de Carvajal, *Anales breves,* p. 541 note.
32. López Martínez, *Santa Hermandad,* p. 8. Original source not cited.
33. AGS Diversos, leg. 8, fol. 1.
34. The first document in which this name is found was issued at the General Assembly of San Miguel del Pino on December 19, 1476, cited in López Martínez, *Santa Hermandad,* p. 11.
35. One hundred and fifty horsemen with attendant footsoldiers. Serrano, *Burgos,* pp. 171 f.. Original source: AMB, 1476, fol. 7.
36. Serrano, *Burgos, p.* 177. Original source: AMB, 1476, fols. 44, 45.
37. Pulgar, *Crónica Reyes Católicos,* pt. 1, ch. 70.
38. Jerónimo de Zurita y Castro. *Anales de la Corona de Aragón* . . . 6 vols. (Zaragoza, 1562–1580), vol. 4, bk. 20, ch. 21; Biblioteca Nacional, Madrid, MS R22905, "Leyes Nuevas de la Hermandad."
39. Pulgar, *Crónica Reyes Católicos,* pt. 1, ch. 70.
40. Ibid. 41. AGS Diversos, leg. 8, fol. 2. 42. Ibid.
43. Such as archbishoprics, bishoprics, and other traditional divisions in order of decreasing size. AGS Diversos, leg. 8, fol. 1.
44. Ibid., fol. 2. 45. Ibid.
46. This militia, emerging for the first time at Dueñas, will be analyzed in chapter 6.
47. AGS Diversos, leg. 8, fol. 2.
48. Pulgar, *Crónica Reyes Católicos,* pt. 1, ch. 70. Other statutes deal with such offenses as robbery or violence in the countryside; burning of houses; and rape.
49. In the Cortes of 1480, although representation was privileged and restricted, fifteen cities and two towns (Madrid and Valladolid) were represented.
50. AGS Diversos, leg. 8, fol. 2; Serrano, *Burgos,* p. 178. Original source: AMB, 1476, fol. 50.
51. López Martínez, *Santa Hermandad,* p. 11. Original source not cited.
52. Ibid. 53. Palencia, *Crónica Enrique IV,* bk. 28, ch. 6
54. AGS Diversos, leg. 8, fol. 3. 55. Ibid.
56. In Seville the office of *juez ejecutor* was combined in 1479 with the office of *provincial* (created in 1476 to watch over the alcaldes, collect money, and assure justice). The new official was called the *juez ejecutor y provincial del la Hermandad de Sevilla, su tierra y provincia.* López Martínez, *Santa Hermandad,* pp. 93 f.
57. Palencia, *Crónica Enrique IV,* vol. 4, bk. 29, ch. 2.
58. Archivo Municipal de Sevilla, Tumbo de los Reyes Católicos, bk. 1, fols. 139–140.
59. Ibid., fols. 140–146. 60. Ibid., fols. 138v–139.
61. A royal letter dated May 17 from Trujillo indicates that he had already been at work for some time. AMS Tumbo, bk. 1, fol. 179.
62. Diego Ortiz de Zuñiga, *Anales eclesiasticos y seculares de la muy noble y muy leal ciudad de Sevilla* . . . (Madrid, 1677), 202: 379.
63. Palencia, *Crónica Enrique IV,* vol. 4, bk. 28, ch. 6.
64. Ibid.

65. Serrano, *Burgos,* p. 181. Original sources: Archivo Cathedral de Burgos, Libro Rodondo 1477, and AMB, Regimento, 19, fol. 110.
66. Ibid. 67. Ibid. 68. AGS Diversos, leg. 8, fol. 2.
69. Zurita y Castro, *Anales de Aragón,* vol. 4, bk. 20, ch. 21.
70. Ibid.
71. Palencia, *Crónica Enrique IV,* vol. 4, bk. 30, ch. 6.
72. Zurita y Castro, *Anales de Aragón,* vol. 4, bk. 20, ch. 21.
73. Palencia, *Crónica Enrique IV,* vol. 4, bk. 30, ch. 7.
74. Serrano, *Burgos,* p. 182. Original source: AMB, 1478, fol. 26.
75. López Martínez, *Santa Hermandad,* pp. 11 f. Original source not cited.
76. Text of treaty in Antonio de la Torre, ed., *Documentos referentes a las relaciones con Portugal durante el reinado de los Reyes Católicos,* 3 vols. (Valladolid, 1959–1963), 1:254–284.
77. Juana was offered the option of marrying Isabella's son or of entering a convent. She chose a convent in Portugal where she lived to the age of sixty-nine, calling herself "I, the Queen" to the end of her life.
78. AMS Tumbo, bk. 2, fols. 11v–12v.
79. Ibid., fols. 10–11v. 80. Ibid.
81. Lists were published of the following provinces: Seville, Jerez de la Frontera, Cordova, Jahen, Trujillo, Extremadura; in the bishoprics of Palencia, Coria, Badajoz; and in the lands of the Order of Santiago in Leon. Ibid., fols. 16v–18.
82. Ibid., fols. 14–15v.

Notes to Chapter 3

1. AGS Diversos, leg. 8, fol. 4.
2. Ibid., fol. 2.
3. Galicia, Asturias, Vizcaya, Guipuzcoa, Alava, and the seacoast; lands of duke of Medina Sidonia, marques of Cadiz; villages of Moquer, Palos, Santa Maria del Puerto. Ibid. See also AGS Contaduría del Sueldo, Iª ser., leg. 53, fol. 10, showing amounts contributed 1481–1482. The cities and lands of Seville contributed 1,900,000 maravedís, the bulk of the funds.
4. AGS Diversos, leg. 8, fol. 4.
5. Pulgar, *Crónica Reyes Católicos,* pt. 2, ch. 139; Alonso de Palencia, *Guerra de Granada,* tr. into Castilian from the Latin by Antonio Paz y Mélia (Madrid, 1909), bk. 3.
6. Serrano, *Burgos,* p. 184. Original source: AMB, 1483, fols. 46, 52, 53.
7. Diego Clemencín, *Elogio de la reina Católica Doña Isabel,* in *Memorias de la Real Academia de la Historia,* no. 6 (Madrid, 1821), p. 137.
8. Clemencín, *Elogio de la reina,* pp. 137 f.

9. This book is sometimes called the "Code of Cordova" because it was confirmed by the monarchs in that city on July 7, 1486. The only existent version of the 1485 laws is a copy printed in Burgos in 1527, the "Leyes Nuevas de la Hermandad," BN, MS R22905.

10. Escaped criminals were still punishable by the brotherhood whatever the original cause of sentencing. Ibid.

11. Ibid.

12. Royal letters issued from Alcalá, January 14, 1486, and Salamanca January 25, 1487, cited by López Martínez, *Santa Hermandad,* p. 98. Original source not given.

13. AGS Sello, August 1486, fol. 31.

14. Ibid., December 1487, fol. 170.

15. Ibid., February 1491, fol. 204.

16. Ibid., June 1489, fol. 151.

17. Ibid., August 1489, fol. 205.

18. Ibid., August 1488, fol. 51.

19. Yet even in 1478 the queen had to threaten the city with reprisals when for a time it refused to pay its contribution. Serrano, *Burgos,* pp. 182 f. Original source: royal letter from Cordova dated November 13, 1478, in the AMB, 1478, fol. 72.

20. The Reyes Católicos attempted to end this practice. Serrano, *Burgos,* p. 12.

21. Serrano, *Burgos,* pp. 184ff. Original source: AMB, 1483, fols. 46, 52, 53.

22. Ibid., p. 186. Original source: AMB, 1485, fol. 4.

23. Ibid., p. 187. Original source: AMB, 1486, fol. 77.

24. AMS Tumbo, bk. 2, fols. 14–15v; 164v–165.

25. Benito Ruano, *Toledo,* pp. 124 f.

26. The problem of dates is compounded by the right granted the crown in 1485 to call these gatherings when convenient to the monarchs. "Leyes Nuevas de la Hermandad," BN, MS R22905.

27. López Martínez, *Santa Hermandad,* p. 16. Original source: royal letter of April 30, 1492, from Barcelona.

28. Ibid.   29. AMS Tumbo, bk. 4, fol. 204.

30. López Martínez, *Santa Hermandad,* p. 16. Original source not cited.

31. AMS Tumbo, bk. 4, fols. 420v–421.

32. Ibid., fols. 283–284.   33. Ibid., fols. 355–365v.

34. Ibid., fols. 420–421.

35. The 1496 book of ordinances was incorporated in the sixteenth century into a digest, the *Novísima recopilación de las leyes de España* as bk. 35, now in vol. 5 of *Leyes Españolas* (Madrid, 1867).

36. Clemencín, *Elogio de la reina,* p. 183.

37. Juan Ramírez, ed., *Las pragmaticas del Reyno* (Seville, 1520), pp. 84v–86v. Copy in AMS Tumbo, bk. 5, fols. 152–154. Condensed version in *Novísima recopilación,* bk. 35.

38. Ibid.

Notes to Chapter 4

1. Garrett Mattingly, *Catharine of Aragon* (Boston, 1941), p. 51.
2. Benito Ruano, *Toledo*.   3. Azcona, *Isabel*.
4. Ibid., pp. 269, 283, 292.
5. J. A. Maravall, "The Origins of the Modern State," *Cuadernos de historia mundal* (1961), 6:800 f.
6. Jaime Vicens Vives, *Manual de historia económica de. España* (Barcelona, 1959), p. 270.
7. Jaime Vincens Vives, ed., *Historia social y económica de España y América*, 5 vols. (Barcelona, 1957–1959), 2:464; Lynch, *Cpain Under The Habsburgs*, p. 22.
8. Vicens Vives, *Historia social y económica*, 2:422 f.
9. Vicens Vives, *Manual de historica económica*, p. 268.
10. Vicens Vives, *Historia social y económica*, 2:418; Elliot, *Imperial Spain*, p. 102.
11. Vicens Vives, *Historia social y económica*, 2:439 f; Lynch, *Spain Under the Habsburgs*, p.13.
12. Vicens Vives. *Historia social y económica*, 2:438 f; Lynch, *Spain Under the Habsburgs*, p. 12.
13. Alvaro de Zuñiga, count of Palencia, Diego Hurtado de Mendoza, marques of Santillana, and Pedro Fernández de Velasco, count of Haro. Azcona, *Isabel*, pp. 119 ff. Original source: AHN, Fondo Osuna, leg. 1860, fol. 26.
14. Palencia, *Crónica Enrique IV*, vol. 5, bk. 24, ch. 6.
15. *La Guardia Civil* (Madrid, 1858), p. 323; Clemencín, *Elogio de la reina*, p. 140.
16. Text of petition in Clemencín, *Elogio de la reina*, p. 140.
17. Ibid.
18. Pulgar, *Crónica Reyes Católicos*, pt. 1, ch. 70.   19. Ibid.
20. Also included are church and monastic land and property of the orders of Calatrava, Acantara, and San Juan. AMS Tumbo, bk. 5, fols. 28–29.
21. AGS Sello, leg. 8, fol. 1.
22. This inequality was only slightly lessened in 1498 when the salaries were raised to 30,000 for the aristocrat and 20,000 for the townsman. AMS Tumbo, bk. 5, fol. 204.
23. AGS Diversos, leg. 8, fol. 8.
24. Pulgar, *Crónica Reyes Católicos*, pt. 1, ch. 70.
25. An undated memorial containing a chapter apparently proposed at Dueñas, but not incorporated in the first book. It may have been sent to different nobles after the assembly. AGS Diversos, leg. 8, fol. 10.
26. Pulgar, *Crónica Reyes Católicos*, pt. 1, ch. 70.
27. Ibid.; Puyol y Alonso (*Las hermandades*, p. 99) takes this to mean only for the term set at Dueñas. In 1484, however, we find another letter for exemption, this time for hidalgos of Galicia. AGS Sello, December 1480, fol. 80.

28. AGS Sello, November 1476, fol. 791.
29. Letter to the church of Leon, in AGS Sello, August 1490, fol. 326.
30. Undated documents in the Archivo General de Simancas, Patronato Real, legs. 16, 39, 59.
31. "Leyes Nuevas de la Hermandad," BN, MS R22905.
32. Azcona, *Isabel*, p. 337 note. Original source: Secret Vatican Archives, Rome, Registra Vaticana 685, fols. 406–407v.
33. AGS Sello, December 1484, fol. 80; May 1488, fol. 133; September 1488, fol. 204; May 1490, fols. 141, 161.
34. For example: R. B. Merriman, *The Rise of the Spanish Empire in the Old World and in the New*, 4 vols. (New York, 1918–1934), 2:103; Puyol y Alsonso, *Las hermandades*, p. 93; Mariéjol, *Spain of Ferdinand and Isabella*, pp. 15 f.
35. A term of justification for the assault on the fortress of the Navas in 1476 and the assault upon the castles of Castronuño, Cubillas, Cantalapiedra, and Siete Iglesias in 1477 that protected Juana's city of Toro. Palencia, *Crónica Enriques IV*, vol. 4, bk. 28, ch. 2; Pulgar, *Crónica Reyes Católicos*, pt. 1, ch. 85.
36. AGS Diversos, leg. 8, fol. 3.
37. AGS Sello, August 1476, fol. 567.
38. Ibid., December 1480, fol. 78.
39. Ibid., August 1477, fol. 83 (count of Salinas); October 1486, fol. 127 (count of Medellin); October 1486, fol. 93 (count of Lemos).
40. AGS Diversos, leg. 8, fol. 1; "Leyes Nuevas de la Hermandad," BN, MS R22905; *Novísima recopilación*, bk. 35.
41. AGS Diversos, leg. 8, fol. 3; "Leyes Nuevas de la Hermandad," BN MS R22905; *Novísima recopilación*, bk. 35.

Notes to Chapter 5

1. AGS Diversos, leg. 8, fol. 1–4.
2. Elliot, *Imperial Spain*, p. 71.
3. "Leyes Nuevas de la Hermandad," BN, MS R22905.
4. AMS Tumbo, bk. 3, fols. 103–104.
5. The first use of this formula dates from February 1490. Ibid., fols. 328–331.
6. For example, in 1485 we find a circular letter from the Council addressed to brotherhood judges asking them to look for some thieves, as requested of the royal court by the head judge of Guadalajara. AGS Sello, December 1485, fol. 40.
7. AMS, Actas Capitulares, 1487.
8. AGS Diversos, leg. 8, fol. 1.
9. Serrano, *Burgos*, p. 187. Original source: AMB, 1486, fol. 77.
10. AGS Diversos, leg. 8, fol. 1.
11. Mentioned in undated letter by D. Tomás González. AGS Diversos, leg. 8, fol. 10.
12. In the bills of the brotherhood between August 15, 1490 and

August 15, 1492 is a notation that 1,157,000 maravedís were given
to the bishop of Avila "for the dispatch of the Admiral." Archivo
General de Simancas, Contaduría mayor de cuentas, 1ª época, leg.
134; Azcona, *Isabel*, p. 674.

13.   S. E. Morison, *Admiral of the Ocean Sea*, 2 vols. (Boston, 1942),
1:137 f.

14.   Beneyto Pérez, *Historia de la administración española*, p. 328;
Lynch, *Spain Under the Habsburgs*, p. 10; Elliot, *Imperial Spain*,
pp. 68 ff.

15.   The Ordinances of Fuenterrabía of May 4, 1463 and September 5,
1463 remained in effect through the reign. AGS Diversos, leg. 8,
fol. 5.

16.   AGS Diversos, leg. 8, fol. 5. The brotherhood consisted of the brotherhoods of Alava, with the principal city of Vitoria, and the villages
of Salvatierra, Miranda, Pancorbo, and smaller towns. Henry IV
revived and reformed the league on May 4, 1473 from Miranda.
The organization of the league under Ferdinand and Isabella was
similar to that of Castile, except that in addition to alcaldes, each
area selected two commissaries *(comisarios)* to govern the police.

17.   Azcona, *Isabel*, p. 339 note. Original source: Archivo General de
la Corona de Aragón, Barcelona, Registros de chancillería, 3664,
fols. 379v–380.

18.   The Holy Brotherhood in Aragon was formally eliminated in 1510.
The principal study on the brotherhood in Aragon makes no mention of cooperation with the Castilian Council. See P. A. Muñoz
Casayús, "Las Hermandades en Aragón: Introducción al estudio
general de las hermandades," *Universidad* (Zaragoza, 1927),
4:669–723, and in the same issue "Los capítulos de la Santa Hermandad de Aragón," pp. 905–959.

19.   Jaime Peres Unzueta, *El sometent a traves de la Història* (Barcelona, 1924), pp. 118 ff.

Notes to Chapter 6

1.   Pulgar, *Crónica Reyes Católicos*, pt. 1, ch. 70.

2.   The staff assigned to brotherhood duties was elastic. When more
help was needed, ordinary royal officials were assigned. Rodrigo de
Ulloa, another chief accountant *(contador mayor)* at times aided
Quintanilla on the queen's orders. Antonio Blázquez y Delgado-
Aguilera, *Bosquejo histórico de la administración militar española*
(Madrid, 1891), p. 88.

3.   Serrano, *Burgos*, pp. 213 f; López Martínez, *Santa Hermandad*,
p. 11.

4.   Ibid.   5.   AMS Tumbo, bk. 5, fols. 28–29.

6.   The Registrada del Sello in Simancas, and the books of Tumbo in
the Municipal Archive of Seville are crowded with tax admonishments. These letters, usually in response to requests from unsuccess-

ful local tax officials that the Council take a hand in collection, are explicit as to the required payment that is to be made.

7. AGS Sello, January 1488, fol. 196; March 1491, fol. 309; AMS Tumbo, bk. 4, fols. 320–321.

8. AGS Sello, April 1486, fol. 106 (Jews of Castile); July 1490, fol. 62 (Mercia); March 1491, fol. 62 (Cáceres), fol. 90 (1. Mercia, 2. Cáceres).

9. Ibid., July 1490, fol. 62 (Moors of Mercia).

10. The first chapter of a memorial presented at the Cortes of Toledo in 1480. AGS Diversos, leg. 8, fol. 1039.

11. See Octavio Gill Farrés, *Historia de la moneda española* (Madrid, 1959); Vicens Vives, *Historia social y económica,* 2:43 ff. E. J. Hamilton, *American Treasure and the Price Revolution in Spain, 1501–1650* (Cambridge, Mass., 1934), pp. 50 f; Morison, *Admiral,* 2:185.

12. AGS Diversos, leg. 8, fol. 2.

13. Letter lifting the contribution, July 29, 1498. AMS Tumbo, bk. 5, fols. 152–154.

14. A census undertaken by Quintanilla in 1492 determined that Castile had 1,500,000 households. The maximum yearly projection after 1485 could have been 270,000,000 maravedís, but the Council only obtained one quarter of this amount. Further research is necessary to determine how much was raised at all levels. The municipal share of collections in Ciudad Real, for example, ran three times the amount it gave to the Council. It would appear, however, that all funds collected fell short of the theoretical maximum, considering the number of tax-exempt personages and the concession to seignoral power that subject peasants paid not by household but by low lump-sum payments.

    Memorandum from Quintanilla cited by P. G. Edge, "Early Population Records in Spain," *Metron: International Review of Statistics* (Rome, 1932), vol. 9, no. 3–4, pp. 229 ff; AGS Contaduría mayor, 1ª época, legs. 128, 134; AGS Diversos, leg. 8, fol. 8; *Libro de Cuentas* for 1491–1492, unbound account book in AHN, Seccion de Diversos, leg. 32, no. 2 (Santa Hermandad Vieja de Ciudad Real, Cuentas).

15. AGS Contaduría mayor, 1ª época, leg. 128.

16. This assessment was 1,300,000 for the city, plus 300,000 for its territories. AMS Tumbo, bk. 2, fols. 11v–12v (1479); fols. 331–332 (1484); bk. 5, fols. 28–29 (1496); fols. 81–83 (1497).

17. AMS, Actas Capitulares, February 4, 1480.

18. AGS Contaduría del Sueldo, 1ª ser., leg. 53.

19. AGS Contaduría mayor, 1ª época, leg. 128.

20. AMS Tumbo, bk. 5, fols. 28–29.   21. Ibid., fols. 81–83.

22. Serrano, *Burgos,* p. 184; López Martínez, *Santa Hermandad,* p. 52.

23. AMS Actas Capitulares, December 22, 1487.

24. Ibid., June 22, 1478.   25. Ibid.

26. AMS Actas Capitulares, July 7, 1487.   27. Ibid.

120   THE COUNCIL OF THE SANTA HERMANDAD

28. AMS Mayordomazgo-Carpeta, 1477–1479.
29. AMS Tumbo, bk. 3, fols. 460–461.
30. Ibid., fols. 144v–146.
31. Serrano, *Burgos,* p. 173. Original source: AMB, 1476, fol. 17.
32. AGS Sello, March 1487, fol. 44; June 1489, fol. 97; July 1490, fol. 224.
33. AGS Sello, 1491; January, fol. 273; February, fols. 93, 121, 234; March, fols. 341, 419, 554; April, fol. 132; May, fol. 24.
34. AMS Tumbo, bk. 4, fols. 418–420.
35. Letter issued from Valladolid on February 22, 1496. Document #13 in appendix of Clemencín, *Elogio de la reina,* pp. 603–605.
36. New taxes were ordered to take their place. BN, Hermandad Vieja de Toledo, MS 13030.
37. AMS Tumbo, bk. 5, fols. 174v–175.
38. Ibid., fol. 204.   39. Ibid.. fols. 142–142v.
40. AGS Diversos, leg. 8, fol. 3.   41.Ibid.
42. Ibid.; Pulgar, *Crónica Reyes Católicos,* pt. 2, ch. 139.
43. AGS Libro de Cedulas, leg. 1, fol. 2.
44. AGS Contaduría mayor, 1ª época, leg. 128.
45. AMS Tumbo, bk. 3, fols. 200–201.
46. Yitzhak Baer, *A History of the Jews in Christian Spain,* trans., Louis Schaffman, 2 vols. (New York, 1961), vol. 2, pp. 315 f.
47. Letter of grant of office dated July 12, 1490. AGS Contaduría del Sueldo, 1ª ser., leg. 53, fol. 39. Due to his conversion he stayed on at his post after the expulsion.
48. Baer, *Jews in Christian Spain,* 2:315f.
49. AGS Contaduría del Sueldo, 1ª, leg. 53, fol. 39.
50. "Leyes Nuevas de la Hermandad," BN, MS R22905.
51. AGS Diversos, leg. 8, fol. 8.
52. The brotherhood of Avila was ordered to work with the treasurers of the Bull in 1484. AGS Sello, October 1484, fol. 179.
53. Isabella commanded an alcalde to gather data in 1483 regarding local taxes being levied upon the Mesta flocks. Klein, *The Mesta,* p. 212. Original source: Archive of the Mesta, A-8, Haro 1483.
54. Colmeiro, *Cortes de los antiguos reinos,* 4:3–11.
55. AGS Diversos, leg. 8, fols. 1, 2.
56. AGS Diversos, leg. 8, fol. 1; Pulgar, *Crónica Reyes Católicos,* pt. 1, ch. 70; Palencia, *Crónica Enrique IV,* vol. 5, bk. 24, ch. 6
57. AGS Diversos, leg. 8, fol. 1.   58. Serrano, *Burgos,* p. 180.
59. Sarafín María de Soto, count of Clonard, *Historia orgánica de las armas de infantería y caballería españolas desde la creación del ejército permanente hasta el día,* 16 vols. (Madrid, 1851–1859), 2:166 ff.
60. AGS Sello, April 1477, fol. 103; December 1478, fol. 20.
61. P. J. Stewart, Jr., "The Army of the Catholic Kings: Spanish Military Organization and Administration in the Reign of Ferdinand and Isabella 1474-1516." Ph.D. dissertation, University of Illinois, 1961, p. 36.

62. Pulgar, *Crónica Reyes Católicos,* pt. 1, ch. 70.
63. Throughout the existence of the militia, figures given in chronicles and paymusters concerning troop strength are inexact. In Castile one "lance" consisted of (1) an armored soldier, (2) a page on horseback, and (3) possibly some footsoldiers. One "man-at-arms" had an adjunct with a crossbow and up to four attendants. Stewart, "Army of the Catholic Kings," pp. 147, 148, 204.
64. Figure from Palencia, *Crónica Enrique IV,* vol. 4, bk. 24, ch. 6. Pulgar (*Crónica Reyes Católicos,* pt. 1, ch. 70) gives a vague total of more than 2,000.
65. AGS Diversos, leg. 8, fol. 2.
66. Ibid., fol. 1. 67. Ibid., fol. 2. 68. Ibid.
69. Pulgar, *Crónica Reyes Católicos,* pt. 1, ch. 70.
70. The men were distributed into companies: 140 lancers for the supreme commander, and twenty for the Council president; one company of 130 lancers; three of 110; six of 100; one of eighty; one of forty; and one of twenty lancers. AGS Contaduría del Sueldo, 1ª ser., leg. 53.
71. Ibid. 72. AGS Diversos, leg. 8, fol. 3.
73. Soto, *Historia orgánica,* 2:166 f.
74. Stewart, "Army of the Catholic Kings," p. 292.
75. Azcona, *Isabel,* p. 508. The following May the provincial brotherhood of Seville undertook a census of all available beasts in the city and province to fulfill this commitment for the relief of Alhama. AMS Tumbo, bk. 2, fols. 232v–233v.
76. "Leyes Nuevas de la Hermandad," BN, MS R22905.
77. Serrano, *Burgos,* p. 184.
78. Azcona, *Isabel,* p. 514. 79. Ibid., p. 516.
80. AGS Contaduría del Sueldo, 1ª ser., leg. 53, fol. 3.
81. Azcona, *Isabel,* p. 523. 82. Ibid., p. 524.
83. Royal decree of January 15, 1488 reporting the results of the General Assembly. AGS Contaduría del Sueldo, 1ª ser., leg. 53, fol. 3.
84. Ibid. 85. Soto, *Historia orgánica,* 2:166 f.
86. Ibid. 87. Ibid., p. 68.
88. Jorge Vigón Suero-Díaz, *Historia de la artillería española,* 3 vols. (Madrid, 1947), 1:99 f.
89. Proposal to the General Assembly of Madrid. January 25, 1480. AGC *Contaduría del Sueldo,* 1ª ser., leg. 53, fol. 5.
90. Pulgar, *Crónica Reyes Católicos,* pt. 2, ch. 233.
91. Soto (*Historia orgánica,* 2:165) sees the establishment of a general, or divisional, command already existing at Granada, where all in the armies fought under one command supported by companies of carpenters, gunsmiths, etc. The assessment of Stewart ("Army of the Catholic Kings," p. 209) that no real attempt was made to create divisional commands in the modern sense appears more realistic.
92. The queen mentions in a letter of January 4, 1480 from Toledo

that the Parliament of Delegates was lodged in that city. AMS Tumbo, bk. 2, fols. 14–15.

93. The first such document reviewed deals with a citizen who was imprisoned by an alcalde while on his way to serve in the war with his footsoldiers. AGS Sello, April 1487, fol. 59.

94. Numerous examples in AGS Sello section.

95. Vigón Suero-Diáz (*Historia de la artillería española,* 1:74) cites a royal edict of January 10, 1489 assigning eight million maravedís from brotherhood funds to pay salaries and expenses connected with artillery, as evidence of a separate artillery unit.

96. AGS Contaduría del sueldo, 1ª ser., leg., 53, fol. 3.

97. Soto, *Historia orgánica,* 2:167.

98. Merriman, *Rise of the Spanish Empire,* 2:177.

99. Letter to the sovereigns from Barcelona, May 23, 1493, cited in López Martínez, *Santa Hermandad,* p. 21.

100. Undated memorandum from Quintanilla to the king and queen: text in Rafael Fuertes Arias, *Alfonso de Quintanilla contador mayor de los Reyes Católicos,* 2 vols. (Oviedo, 1909), 1:172 ff. Also in Francisco Barado y Font, *Museo militar: Historia del ejército español . . .* 3 vol. (Barcelona, 1882), 1:372 f, where it is dated 1492.

101. Ibid.

102. Royal letter of May 13, 1495, AMS Tumbo, bk. 4, fols. 420–421.

103. Soto, *Historia orgánica,* 2:249.   104. Ibid.

105. Royal ordinance issued in Tarragona on September 18, 1495, in Ramírez, *Pragmáticas del Reyno,* pp. 83v–84v.

106. Royal decree issued in Valladolid on February 22, 1496, in Clemencín, *Elogio de la reina,* document no. 13 of appendix, pp. 603–605; Soto, *Historia orgánica,* 2:254–257.

107. Jaoquín de Sotto y Montes, "Organización militar de los Reyes Católicos," *Revista de Historia Militar* (Madrid, 1963), vol. 8, no. 14, p. 20; Soto, *Historia orgánica,* 2:257.

108. Stewart, "Army of the Catholic Kings," pp. 193 f.

109. Ibid.

110. Date given by Clemencín, *Elogio de la reina,* p. 183.

111. Maintenance of such a force would have cost 2,815,989 copper reales each month, not considering the wages of superior officers. Stewart, "Army of the Catholic Kings," pp. 193 f.

Notes to Chapter 7

1. Founded in 1262 as Villarreal. Leopoldo Torres Balbás, *Resumen historico del urbanismo en España* (Madrid, 1954), p. 78.

2. Confirmed by Alfonso X in 1258 with its sister cities in the Ancient Royal Brotherhood of Toledo, Talavera, and Villarreal. Paz y Mélia, "Santa Real," p.98.

3. Libro de Cuentas for 1491-1492, unbound account book in AHN,

Seccion de Diversos, leg. 32, no. 2 (Santa Hermandad Vieja de Ciudad Real, Cuentas).

4. Libro de Cuentas, fols. 3, 3v, 4v, 5.
5. Ibid., fol. 5.   6. Ibid., fol. 4v.
7. Paz y Mélia, "Santa Real," p. 120.
8. AHN Diversos, Libro de Cuentas, fols. 6, 8v.
9. Ibid., fols. 12v, 13, 15.
10. "Leyes Nuevas de la Hermandad," BN MS R22905; *Novísima recopilación,* bk. 35.
11. There were also such lesser responsibilities as prohibiting usury and checking that roadside inns observe rates set by the authorities. Ibid.; Pulgar, *Crónica Reyes Católicos,* pt. 1, ch. 70; AMS Tumbo, bk. 1, fols. 310v–311.
12. AHN Diversos, Libro de Cuentas, fol. 3.   13. Ibid., fol 5.
14. Some of the constables had other employment. An innkeeper is identified as a brother in Miguel de Cervantes Saavedra, *The Visionary Gentleman Don Quijote de la Mancha,* trans. Robinson Smith. 2 vols. (New York, 1932), pt. 1, ch. 45.
15. Paz y Mélia, "Santa Real," p. 104; Clemente Palencia Flores, *Museo de La Santa Hermandad de Toledo,* Guias de los Museos de España (Toledo, 1958), pp. 13 f.
16. It might be possible to find a closer connection between the two systems of justice than historical congruence. Castilian settlers of the New World brought a heritage with them that they passed on to American cowboys. Lynn White, Jr., in his provocative essay, "The Legacy of the Middle Ages in the American Wild West" *(Speculum,* April 1965) points out that the medieval world handed on concepts of splintered political authority, the style in which log cabins were built, and artifacts like barbed wire, wagons, and revolvers. Even the word "buckaroo" came from the *vaquero* who rode the Spanish plains. If it could be equally demonstrated that the New World settlers set up equivalents to the hermandades they knew at home, a direct link might be traced.
17. AGS Diversos, leg. 8, fol. 1.
18. AHN Diversos, Libro de Cuentas, fol. 5.
19. Cervantes, *Don Quijote,* pt. 1, ch. 45.
20. AHN Diversos, Libro de Cuentas, fol. 7.   21. Ibid., fol. 7v.
22. These customs were observed until 1505. Paz y Mélia, "Santa Real," p. 120.
23. AHN Diversos, Libro de Cuentas, fol. 7v.   24. Ibid., fol. 8.
25. AGS Libros de cédulas, leg. 1, fol. 2.
26. AHN Diversos, Libro de Cuentas, fols. 6, 9, 16.
27. Ibid., fols. 12v, 15.   28. Ibid., fols. 3v, 15.
29. Ibid., fol. 6v.   30. Ibid., fol. 14.
31. AGS Diversos, leg. 8, fol. 1; "Leyes nuevas de la Hermandad," BN, MS R22905. Despite haste these procedures were a distinct advance over the ancient custom, which Paz y Mélia informs us was to hold the trial after the execution ("Santa Real," p. 120.)

32. AGS Diversos, leg. 8, fol. 4.
33. AHN Diversos, Libro de Cuentas, fols. 6–14.
34. "Leyes Nuevas de la Hermandad," BN, MS R22905.
35. Francisco López de Villalobos, *Los problemas de Villalobos*. . . ., Biblioteca de autores españolas, no. 36 (Madrid, 1855), p. 429.
36. AGS Diversos, leg. 8, fol. 1; "Leyes Nuevas de la Hermandad," BN, MS R22905.
37. Albert Du Boys, *Historia del derecho penal en España* (Madrid, 1878), p. 455
38. "Leyes Nuevas de la Hermandad," BN, MS R22905.
39. Ramírez, *Pragmáticas del reyno*, pp. 84v-86v; *Novísima recopilación*, bk. 35.
40. Cortes of Segovia, December 22, 1532, Colmeiro, *Cortes de los antiguos reinos*, 4:561.
41. AHS Diversos, Libro de Cuentas, fol. 15.
42. In this regard it is of interest that the account book of Ciudad Real for 1491–1492 makes no mention of the Council or any member thereof.
43. Incorporated in a bound folio of letters of privilege for the Brotherhoods of Toledo, Talavera, and Ciudad Real in AHN Diversos, leg. 1, no. 8, (Santa Hermandad de Ciudad Real, Procesos).
44. Ibid.   45. AHN Diversos, Libro de Cuentas, fol. 3.
46. Ibid., fol. 12.   47. Ibid., fol. 15v.
48. AGS Contaduría mayor, 1ª época, leg. 128, no pagination.
49. AHN Diversos, Libro de Cuentas, fols. 4, 10.
50. Letter from Seville issued July 7, 1478. AMS Tumbo, bk. 1, fols. 310–311v.
51. AGS Sello, September 1478, fol. 94; April 1488, fol. 82; May 1489, fol. 208; December 1489, fol. 234.
52. Ibid., September 1478, fol. 55.
53. Ibid., October 1478, fol. 135; September 1489, fol. 359.
54. AGS Diversos, leg. 8, fol. 4.
55. AGS Sello, May 1486, fol. 78.
56. Ibid., January 1488, fol. 151.
57. "Leyes Nuevas de la Hermandad," BN, MS R22905; *Novísima recopilación*, bk. 35.
58. AMS Tumbo, bk. 5, fols. 348–349, June 20, 1500.
59. Cervantes, *Don Quijote*, pt. 1, ch. 10, 23, 45.

Note to Chapter 8

1. Ramírez, *Pragmáticas del Reyno*, pp. 84v–86v. Copy in AMS Tumbo, bk. 5, fols. 152–154.

Bibliography

Archival Material

Spain's archives are rich in unpublished materials of the late fifteenth century. The organization of the materials ranges from excellent in the national repositories to chaotic in some provincial collections. In the chief Castilian archives, the Archivo General de Simancas, copies of Council letters are preserved in the section Registro General del Sello de la Corte; laws and ordinances of the brotherhood are preserved in Diversos de Castilla; uncatalogued fragments of bills are in Contaduría Mayor de Cuentas and Patronato Real; records pertaining to the militia during the Granada War are in Secretaria de Guerra y Marina.

The Archivo Histórico Nacional of Madrid has several important collections. Seccion de Diversos and Codices y Cartularios contain charters, ordinances, and books of account for Ciudad Real, Toledo, and Talavera. The Biblioteca Nacional of Madrid has books of ordinances and laws in the section Hermandad Vieja de Toledo.

The most useful provincial archive for this study was the Archivo Municipal de Sevilla. Seven large volumes of the Tumbos de los Reyes Católicos preserve transcriptions of all royal correspondence with the city from 1477. Proceedings by year of the municipal corporation are found in the Cuadernos de Actas Capitulares.

The Archivo Municipal de Burgos has bound yearly volumes of municipal sessions, which incorporate royal letters read before the city council. Of special interest are the records of the years from 1476 to 1488.

The municipal archives of the city of Toledo have disappointingly few brotherhood papers from the era of the Reyes Católicos. The few privileges and decrees in Toledo's archives are duplicated in the small archives of the Museo de la Santa Hermandad de Toledo, housed in a restored jail house.

Primary sources

Bernáldez, Andrés. *Memorias del reinado de los Reyes Católicos.* Edited with a study by Manuel Gómez-Moreno and Juan de Mata Carriazo. Madrid, 1962.

Carvejal, Lorenzo Galíndez de. *Anales breves del reinado de los Reyes Católicos.* Edited by Cayetano Rosell y López. Biblioteca de autores españoles, no. 70. Madrid, 1878.

Carvejal, Lorenzo Galíndez de. *Cronica de Enrique IV.* Edited with a study by Juan Torres Fontes. Murcia, 1946.

Cervantes Saavedra, Miguel de. *The Visionary Gentleman Don Quijote de la Mancha.* Translated by Robinson Smith. 2 vols. New York, 1932.

Colmeiro, Manuel, ed. *Cortes de los antiquos reinos de León y de Castilla publicados por la Academia de la Historia.* 5 vols. Madrid, 1863–1903.

Enríquez del Castillo, Diego. *Crónica de Rey Don Enrique el Cuarto.* Edited by Cayetano Rosell y López. Biblioteca de autores españoles, no. 70. Madrid, 1878.

Madrid. Biblioteca Nacional. MS R22905. "Leyes Nuevas de la Hermandad." Burgos, 1527.

López de Villalobos, Francisco. *Los problemas de Villalobos . . . .* Edited by Adolfo de Castro v Rossi. Biblioteca de autores españoles, no. 36. Madrid, 1855.

Novísima recopilación de las leyes de España . . . . Laws pertaining to the Holy Brotherhood in *Leyes Españolas.* 6 vols. Madrid, 1867.

Palencia, Alonso de. *Crónica de Enrique IV.* Translated from the Latin to Castilian by Antonio Paz y Mélia. 4 vols. Madrid, 1904–1908.

Palencia, Alonso de. *Guerra de Granada.* Translated from the Latin to Castilian by Antonio Paz y Mélia. Madrid, 1909.

Pulgar, Fernando del. *Crónica de los Reyes Católicos.* Edited with a study by Juan de Mata Carrizao. 2 vols. Madrid, 1943.

Puyol, Julio, ed. *Crónica incompleta de los Reyes Católicos* (1469–1476): *según un manuscrito anómino de su época.* Madrid, 1934.

Ramírez, Juan, ed. *Las pragmáticas del Reyno.* Seville, 1520.

Torre, Antonio de la, ed. *Documentos referentes a las relaciones con*

Portugal durante el reinado de los Reyes Católicos. 3 vols. Valladolid, 1959–1963. Vol. 1.

Secondary Sources

Aguado Bleye, Pedro. *Manual de historia de España.* 3 vols. Madrid, 1954–1956; revised 1959. Vol. 2.

Azcona, Tarsicio de. *Isabel la Católica: Estudio crítico de su vida y su reinado.* Biblioteca de Autores Cristianos, no. 237. Madrid, 1964.

Baer, Yitzhak. *A History of the Jews in Christian Spain.* Translated by Louis Schoffman. 2 vols. New York, 1961. Vol. 2.

Barado y Font, Francisco. *Museo militar: Historia del ejército español* . . . . 3 vols. Barcelona, 1882. Vol. 1.

Beneyto Pérez, Juan. *Historia del la administración española y hispanoamericana.* Madrid, 1958.

Benito Ruano, Eloy. *Toledo en el siglo XV: Vida política.* Madrid, 1961.

Blázquez y Delgado-Aguilera, Antonio. *Bosquejo histórico de la administración militar española.* Madrid, 1891.

Blázquez y Delgado-Aguilera, Antonio. *Historia de la administración militar.* Madrid, 1897.

Clemencín, Diego. *Elogio de la reina Católica Doña Isabel.* Memorias de la Real Academia de la Historia, no. 6. Madrid, 1821.

Du Boys, Albert. *Historia del derecho penal en España.* Madrid, 1878.

Edge, P. G. "Early Population Records in Spain." *Metron: International Review of Statistics.* 9(1932) : 229–249.

Elliot, J. H. *Imperial Spain 1469–1716.* New York, 1964.

Ferrara, Orestes. *Un pleito succesorio: Enrique IV, Isabel de Castilla y La Beltraneja.* Madrid. 1945.

Fuertes Arias, Rafael. *Alfonso de Quintanilla contador mayor de los Reyes Católicos.* 2 vols. Oviedo, 1909.

Gil Farrés, Octavio. *Historia de la moneda española.* Madrid, 1959.

La Guardia Civil. Madrid, 1858.

Haebler, Konrad. "Die Kastilischen Hermandades zur Zeit Heinrichs IV (1454–1474)," *Historische Zeitschrift.* Vol. 56(1904).

Hamilton, E. J. *American Treasure and the Price Revolution in Spain, 1501–1650.* Cambridge, Mass., 1934.

Klein, Julius. *The Mesta: A Study in Spanish Economic History.* Cambridge, 1920.

Lévi-Provencal, Evariste. *Histoire de l'Espagne Musulmane.* 3 vols. Paris, 1953. Vol. 3.

López Martínez, Celestino. *La Santa Hermandad de los Reyes Católicos.*
Seville, 1921.
Lynch, John. *Spain Under the Habsburgs: Empire and Absolutism
1515–1598.* Oxford, 1964.
Marañón, Gregorio. *Ensayo biológico sobre Enrique IV de Castilla y
su tiempo.* Madrid, 1934.
Maravall, J. A. "The Origins of the Modern State," *Cuadernos de
historia mundal.* Vol. 6 (1961).
Mariéjol, J. H. *The Spain of Ferdinand and Isabella.* Translated with
an introduction by B. J. Keen. New Brunswick, N.J., 1964.
Mattingly, Garrett. *Catharine of Aragon.* Boston, 1941.
Merriman, R. B. *The Rise of the Spanish Empire in the Old World
and in the New.* 4 vols. New York, 1918–1934. Vol. 2.
Montalvo y Jardín, Louis de. *Discurso sobre las hermandades de
Castilla . . . .* Madrid, 1862.
Morison, S. E. *Admiral of the Ocean Sea.* 2 vols. Boston, 1942.
Muñoz Casayús, P. A. "Las Hermandades en Aragón: Introducción
al estudio general de las Hermandades," *Universidad* 4(1927):
669–723.
Muñoz, Casayús, P. A. "Los capítulos de la Santa Hermandad de
Aragón," *Universidad* 4(1927):905–959.
Ortiz de Zúñiga, Diego. *Anales eclesiásticos y seculares de la muy noble
y muy leal ciudad de Sevilla . . . .* Madrid, 1677. Vol. 202.
Palencia Flores, Clemente. *Museo de la Santa Hermandad de Toledo.*
Guias de los Museos de España. Toledo, 1958.
Paz y Mélia, Antonio. *El cronista Alonso de Palencia: su vida y su
obras . . . .* Madrid, 1914.
Paz y Mélia, Antonio. "La Santa Real Hermandad Vieja y la Nueva
Hermandad General del Reino." *Revista de Archivos, Bibliotecas
y Museos* 1(1897):97–108.
Peres Unzueta, Jaime. *El sometent a traves de la Historia.* Barcelona,
1924.
Puyol y Alonso, Julio. *Las Hermandades de Castilla y León.* Madrid,
1913.
Serrano, L. P. *Los Reyes Católicos y la ciudad de Burgos: desde 1451
a 1492.* Madrid, 1943.
Soto, Sarafín María de, count of Clonard. *Historia orgánica de las
armas de infantería y caballería españolas desde la creación del
ejército permanente hasta el día.* 16 vols. Madrid, 1851–1859.
Vol. 2.
Sotto y Montes, Joaquin de. "Organización militar de los Reyes
Católicos," *Revista de Historia Militar* 8(1963):7–47.
Stewart, P. J., Jr. "The Army of the Catholic Kings: Spanish Military

Organization and Administration in the Reign of Ferdinand and Isabella 1474–1516." Ph.D. dissertation, University of Illinois, 1961.

Stiges, J. B. *Enrique IV y La Excelente Señora: llamada vulgarmente Doña Juana la Beltraneja*. Madrid, 1913.

Suárez Fernández, Luis. "Evolución histórica de las hermandades castellanas," *Cuadernos de historia de España* 16(1951):5–45.

Suárez Fernández, Luis. *Nobleza y monarquía: puntos de vista sobre la historia Castilla de siglo XV*. Valladolid, 1959.

Torres Balbás, Leopoldo, *Resumen historico del urbanismo en España*. Madrid, 1954.

Valencia, J. F. D. *La guerra civil a la muerta de Enrique IV: Zamora Toro, Castronuño*. Zamora, 1929.

Vicens Vives, Jaime. *Historia crítica de la vida y reinado de Fernando II de Aragón*. Zaragoza, 1962.

Vicens Vives, Jaime. *Historia social y económica de España y América*. 5 vols. Barcelona, 1957–1959. Vol. 2.

Vicens Vives, Jaime. *Manual de historia económica de España*. Barcelona, 1959.

Vigón Suero-Díaz, Jorge. *El ejército de los Reyes Católicos: Hay un estilo militar de vida*. Collecion de libros de actualidad politica, no. 13. Madrid, 1953.

Vigón Suero-Díaz, Jorge. *Historia de la artilleria española*. 3 vols. Madrid, 1947. Vol. 1.

White, Lynn, Jr. "The Legacy of the Middle Ages in the American Wild West." *Speculum* 40 (April 1965).

Zurita y Castro, Jerónimo de. *Anales de la Corona de Aragón*. . . . 6 vols. Zaragoza, 1562–1580. Vol. 4.

Index